A PHENOMENAL
JOURNEY

CYNTHIA MCGEE BURTON, M.A.

Who are your intended readers?

How did or do your syblings feel about your book?

This Stuff's Working! Publishing

www.aphenomenaljourney.com

ISBN: 978-1-7340963-2-3

DEDICATION

This book is dedicated to the legacy of my beloved parents
Willie and Eddie McGee, to my siblings, to all of our children
and grandchildren, to Aunt Marie, Aunt Mary Frances,
and to the generations to come.

TABLE OF CONTENTS

FOREWORD

Dear Reader,

I wrote this book during a difficult time in my life. In the year 2020 and the beginning of 2021, I found myself emotionally holding on to my beautiful family's history and, at the same time, trying to maintain a tight grip on our free nation, which was ripping apart at the seams real-time, right in front of my eyes. We were in the middle of a worldwide, out-of-control COVID-19 coronavirus pandemic, a rise in racial injustice, political warfare, and an economic recession. The US economy shut down for almost a year in hopes of controlling the virus. Students from preschool to college were learning at home in virtual classrooms. Socialization, churches, sports events had all come to a complete halt while the local government worked diligently on ways to bring them back to a new normal. Mass shootings, suicide, depression, drug abuse, and divorce were all on the rise. Police were murdering black men like George Floyd, and all of it was captured in broad daylight by personal cell phone video cameras and police body cameras. Such incidents caused a burst of worldwide protests and riots. The community destruction was likened to the Civil Rights Era and the 1990's Rodney King riots. Asians were becoming a target of deadly hate crimes due to the negative narrative related to the origin of the COVID-19 coronavirus in Japan. We had a historical insurrection that caused death at the US capitol while our country was in the middle of confirming the votes of our new president Joe Biden and our first Black female Vice President, Kamala Harris. Jim Crow era voter suppression re-emerged. The most devastating part of all was that our country lost over 500,000 (and counting) precious Americans from the virus. Unfortunately, one of them was my FATHER.

While grieving my father's death, I began to recount the process of grieving for my mother, who had passed over 20 years earlier. It became overwhelming, and I needed a way to get through this part of my life journey. So, I thought about how my parents raised me. I began to grow a deeper appreciation for the role every adult has in the life of a child. My parents had to navigate through life during the civil rights era. They intentionally equipped me with the tools that helped me make it successfully to my senior years. Difficulties and challenges are inevitable parts of life. As the life cycle continues, prayerfully, someone you may have intentionally or unintentionally impacted will live with that special part of you in them.

As you read A Phenomenal Journey, I hope you find a purpose or reason to share a special part of you with someone. I also pray that you share your story so this special part of you will

I heard your voice

2

live on forever. My next book, Destiny Awaits, continues to tell my story of challenges amidst other celebrations. I live my life in awe of God and with a special part of my parents alive within me. So, I share a special part of them with whoever reads my life stories in this book. My parents taught me to give of myself in order to make something or someone appreciate the life they are blessed to live. I pray that this gift I am giving to you will empower you to think about how you will live out your life's journey. Make an intentional effort to look inside the bags you carry. Decide if they are the right bags for you and if you can share them with others.

Blessings,
Cynthia McGee Burton

This foward inspiried me

FRONT PAGE OF THE HONOLULU STAR BULLETIN ON APRIL 30, 1958

A JOURNEY BEGINS

First-Born Daughter

"Policemen Act as Midwives As Baby Girl Is Born In Car" stated the Honolulu newspaper's front page on April 30, 1958.

My mother, Eddie McGee, presented a microfiche copy of the newspaper to me on my 18th birthday. As I read it, my mind sank into the deepest part of my imagination, entering the scene in an out-of-body experience.

I pictured myself as my dad, Airman Willie McGee, speeding down the road in Honolulu, Hawaii, in the middle of the night, trying to get my mother to the military hospital as she was screaming with each spasm of her labor contractions.

"Willie, the baby is coming!" she cried out, reaching the maximum threshold of her pain tolerance.

I did not know you were born in the car.

Dad slammed on the gas pedal and accelerated to the highest speed possible, hoping to make it to the hospital in time.

Then to his surprise, flashing red and blue lights appeared in his rear-view mirror, with a siren ringing out in concert.

It would be nice to imagine that the police would simply alert the world that I was near arrival and offer my mom and dad a colorful escort to the hospital, but no. That's not how encounters with the police went for Black people in the late 50s.

Instead, dad had to make a split decision--stop for the police or continue his mission to get mom and me to the hospital. Without a second thought, he continued towards the hospital at even a higher speed. Even in my imagination, I can feel dad snapping back against the seat as he floored the gas.

The police must have called for backup because soon, the sirens became louder. The blue and red lights flashed brighter. Then, dad heard a demanding voice call out from a loudspeaker, "Slow down and pull over NOW!"

With mom's moans beginning to sound weary and with the fear of their baby not making it into the world alive and healthy, dad realized the police were closing in on him. He quickly pulled over to the side of the road and stopped at an intersection.

Two police officers approached the car. I envisioned dad's hands gripping the steering wheel as he held his breath. I could feel his heart pounding in his chest and sweat dripping down his forehead. One of them shined a bright flashlight into my dad's face through the driver's side window.

"MY WIFE IS ABOUT TO HAVE A BABY!" Dad called out angrily before the cop could even speak.

The other police officer peered into the back window and observed that my arrival was indeed impending.

"Willie, she's coming!" mom yelled.

I can just see dad springing into action. He jumped out of the front seat, opened the back door, stepped in front of the police officer, and extended his hands to support my delivery as more police cars arrived on the scene.

While one police officer radioed for the ambulance, another was at my mom's head, and two others were holding her legs as she gave her final push, sending me into the loving arms of my daddy. I exited my out-of-body experience, still staring at the microfiche clipping, thanking God that all of us had survived that incident with the police against all odds.

Made me cry because
you dad could have been
killed but God not man
nor Police prevailed!

COVER STORY

Policemen Act as Midwives As Baby Girl Is Born in Car

A young Air Force wife gave birth to a girl in a car early today at North King and Kalihi Streets—with two Honolulu policemen serving as midwives.

Airman Willie McGee of the 16th Communications Squadron, Hickam Air Force Base, was taking his wife, Edie, to a hospital in their car, going at high speed and disregarding red lights.

Motor Patrolman Roland Kim halted the speeding auto at 1 a.m. and radioed headquarters for a City-County ambulance.

When the ambulance, bringing nurse Kapiolani Nakahanohano, reached the scene a few minutes later, the blessed event had already occurred, with Officers Kim and Boyd Andrade (both fathers) in complete command of the situation.

Mrs. McGee and daughter were taken to Kapiolani Maternity Hospital—both in good condition.

Whites Took credit

My mom said she could not hold me for several weeks after I was born because the[2] medical staff had to keep me in the hospital. My lungs were so filled with mucus that it was difficult for me to breathe on my own. When I was doing better, they brought me home but monitored my breathing patterns closely.

Dad said he waited a long time for me to open my eyes. He would wonder why I wouldn't look at anyone even as they called out my name, held me close, and made soft cooing sounds to intrigue me. I just wasn't interested in checking out my surroundings.

Policemen Act as Midwives as Baby Girl Is Born in Car." Honolulu Star-Bulletin, 30 April 1958, p.1

Ha you hate possums

I believe I was playing possum to get extra attention and time to solidify my place and prepare myself for the role I would take as the first-born daughter in the McGee family. I grew to love my family beyond measure in loyalty, care, and responsibility.

I am the second born of four children and the first of three daughters. I carried deep love and respect for my family and enjoyed my life experience as a McGee. Even though it is a government name, for me, it represents a human experience. My parents intentionally put time and effort into creating that experience, setting a standard of living that far exceeded my peers.

I was an Air Force military brat. Dad always taught us that being born in America was a privilege. To this day, I respect that to the fullest. I carry a lot of personal commitment to being the best daughter to my parents and my siblings' best sister. My consciousness sets precedence to doing for others well before doing for myself. Life in my skin has been full of challenges that only I could face and overcome.

I've traveled along my journey with bags pre-packed with an expectation of what is ahead. There were many unexpected beginnings in my life that happened quickly, allowing me no time to pack a bag for them. So, I've also carried empty bags, ready to be filled while living in the moment. I have bags I had to unpack based on unexpected cancellations and extended layovers. All of the bags I've carried give depth to my life experiences. My bags hold these moments in time worth sharing in a book. Everyone has a story to tell and a journey to take, and a destiny to fulfill. Never take for granted that you don't have a story to tell. We're all on a phenomenal journey called life. We all have bags.

My journey is not greater or lesser than yours. It's just mine, and I want to share it with you. Why now? Well, now that both my loving parents have transitioned, I want to memorialize their legacy by sharing how they gave four Black children the tools, ambition, and passion for living their best lives. We were not rich nor poor. We were not on welfare, nor did we live in the projects. We never went to sleep without a roof over our heads. We did not experience the life of criminality, drug and alcohol abuse, or other types of abuse in our home.

My mom and dad are now together in their heavenly home. Now it is time for me to honor their legacy and begin to share the stories of my life with them. My prayer is that this book will make you laugh and sometimes even shed a tear of joy or sadness as you learn from my lessons and reflect on your own. I pray that my life experiences give you the desire to live out your destiny and exercise your right as a citizen of this country to be fully present in whatever space God places you. Because it is then and only then that you will have the opportunity to take full advantage of celebrating the day you were born. Later, you define your purpose, understand being divinely created by God and why you even exist on this earth. I have. So, get a cup of coffee or tea, prop your feet up and prepare to begin a phenomenal journey that starts in these pages. Across the series, we will cover the span of my 62 years of life and counting.

All the roads on my journey have not been smooth. These pages contain both positive emotion and overwhelmingly sad moments. My trips and travels have led me to this time in my life without my parents. These moments are worth reliving; my story is worth telling. I know this will be a phenomenal journey for you too. I encourage you to grab the essentials you feel you need from items in my bags and pack them into your own.

When Willie Met Eddie

My mother and father met in Texas when she was 18, and he was 20 years old. Mom was walking home one day when she saw my dad drive by in a red Chevy with a white convertible top. "When our eyes met," mom said, "it was love at first sight." I believe dad first fell in lust and then in love. Mom was a beautiful, shapely African-American young lady, who stood five feet, four inches tall. She had high-yellow skin and jet-black hair that was pressed and curled, hanging around her neckline. Her smile, framed by plump, perfectly shaped lips, was accented with deep dimples on both sides of her cheeks. Squinty brown eyes captured her joy for life.

Dad pulled over and stopped, compelled by an urge not to let mom pass him. As he exited the car and approached her, I can see that moment in my mind just as clearly as I had seen my own birth story. Dad's eyes lowered down to mom's minimal height, while mom's eyes took in **ALL** six feet, four and a half inches of dad. Her eyes climbed up his slim, fit stature. She noted his half-cocked smile of confidence, his dark, dreamy

Very Vivid

brown eyes, and his neatly trimmed haircut. Yes, love at first sight!

Dad was in the Air Force, stationed in Waco, Texas. He was quite the ladies' man! Mom was intrigued by his intelligence and independent desire to accomplish a legacy that far surpassed the family he had left behind.

My paternal grandparents both passed away when dad was very young. My dad's oldest sister raised him. Dad often called himself a loner. He defined himself as an independent, self-motivated achiever. He vowed to depend only on himself and lived that way for all of his days.

During his early teenage years, dad picked cotton for a sharecropper. One day, dad walked off the field, believing that his destiny was to live a better life. He refused to conform to the restraints of being a sharecropper. Dad held his thumb out, hoping and praying. Then he hitchhiked a ride from a White man in a white truck who stopped and offered him a ride to the next town. I believe this man was an angel.

Dad found the military recruiter's office and requested the test needed to enter the Air Force. He loved airplanes and aspired to be a pilot. Dad lived homeless on the streets and studied for his exam under a streetlight. Soon he aced the test and enlisted in the Air Force at age 19.

My mom was the oldest of 11 siblings. She took her responsibility of caring for her sisters and brothers seriously. Her parents were still alive when my parents met. They were poor and sometimes struggled to provide for their family. Mom yearned to experience life beyond the city of Waco, and dad offered her the opportunity. In 1957, dad and mom got married in Texas. They soon welcomed my only brother Edwin Leroy to their union.

Soon after Edwin was born, dad got orders to report to California for transport to Hawaii. My mom rode with my dad to California, joined by my maternal grandfather, great grandfather, my Aunt Marie, her daughter, and my infant brother. It was a family affair! Dad went to Hawaii early to set up housing for his family. Mom's family asked dad to let mom and brother stay with them until his assignment in Hawaii was complete. The request made dad furious. He knew what it felt like not to be raised by a father. He wasn't about to let that happen to his son. "Give me my boy! He's coming with my wife!" He demanded, insisting that my mom pack up her things. She and my brother were to join him on the Air Force base as soon as he secured housing. My mom was scared to death on the flight to Hawaii. It was her first flight. However, she said her fear dissipated with the thought of knowing she was going to be with the love of her life. Our family grew by two while in Hawaii. I was born next, then two years later, my sister Esther was born. By the time we left Hawaii in 1960, we were a family of five and headed to Oklahoma City, Oklahoma.

Military Brat

Living as a middle-class military brat in a Christian household in an African-American family during the end of the civil rights era presented me with challenges, lessons, and privileges that I appreciate and honor to this day.

When we arrived in Oklahoma City, we moved into a green three-bedroom house on the corner of a clean neighborhood. There was a creek running along the back of it. My brother and I would often go there to catch crawdads, tadpoles, and frogs. Ewww! I hardly enjoyed doing it, but if my brother said, "Let's go" then I would go without question. I simply wanted to be wherever he was and do whatever he was doing, even if it made my stomach quiver with disgust.

My father had a TV repair shop. I loved to hang out there with him and help sort the TV tubes, which laid in rows of white cardboard boxes that lined the countertops. Several gutted televisions with wires of various colors hanging out of them scattered all around the shop. It resembled a small warehouse filled with square-headed robots whose detached bodies needed a reboot of electrical shock to function again.

My father was a mechanical engineer in the Air Force. That made him a genius in my mind. His service field was radar missile tracking, so most of the time we were stationed in remote areas of the country so that he could work inside of these huge radar bubbles to track the actions of our foreign enemies.

To me, my dad was the most handsome man in the universe. I loved to watch him complete the finishing touches of getting dressed in his Air Force uniform--putting on his shiny, black shoes, cinching his belt around his slender waist, and tightening his tie around his strong neckline, and sliding his long arms into his military coat while tugging at the cuff of his light blue dress shirt so it would extend just below the arm of his coat sleeve. Then he slowly buttoned his coat up to the very top of his chest. Then he would drag his large hands in a swooping downward motion on each side to secure a fitted look. Straightening up his military medals and ribbons and then finally adjusting his hat in a slight angle that defined his style of class and dignity. He would tilt his head, drop his right shoulder, then head toward the door, grabbing his briefcase and keys. With a nod to the family, he would say, "Ok, see ya soon."

I loved how it felt to come home from school each day and greet my mom and then wait on pins and needles to see my dad walk through the door in his Air Force uniform. When "soon" finally came--and it always seemed like forever--my mom would announce his arrival. Immediately, I would rush to the door to greet him with a warm welcome. I longed to receive a loving hug from him that assured me that he had missed his daughter all day long as I had missed him. But that never happened as a child, that I can remember. He wasn't that type of dad. He had a different way of expressing love. He didn't share physical love, but I never questioned his love. Instead, his response would be, "Hi, kid!" Then he would always throw his hat on my head and walk straight into the kitchen to see what mom had prepared for dinner, sometimes pinching an early bite off of something on the stove. Then, I would watch him tilt that right shoulder and glide down the hallway to the bedroom to change into something comfortable for dinner. When dad came home from work, my family transitioned from mom's free-flowing and interactive nature to a military structured household. My siblings and I served as enlisted troops under Dad's stern but loving command.

McGee Family Core Values

Our family was extremely close. We needed to stick together, especially during the times in which we lived. Dad gave us strict core values as a family that he modeled for us every day:

- First, you are a McGee. Walk with your head up. It forces people to look up to you and not down at you.
- Never call each other out of their name. Disrespect doesn't have a place in our family or our home.
- Establish a personal relationship with God. Learn the Lord's Prayer.
- Living and doing right and helping by loving and respecting your neighbor is Christ-like.
- Never take more from this society than you put into it. Leave this place better than it was when you arrived.
- Get a higher education. It's your ticket to success, and no one can ever take it from you.

Like the scripture Proverb 22:6 says, "Train up a child in the way he should go and when he is old, he will not depart from it."

In Oklahoma, dad was a deacon. We went to church every Sunday. We attended a little white church called the Garden of *what a blessing!*

Prayer Church of God in Christ. Yes, we were Church of God in Christ (COGIC) believers. In my humble, inexperienced mind as a child, that meant that we followed the bible principles in the strictest of terms. We went to church as many days of the week as humanly possible. Paying your tithes faithfully secured you a reserved seat within the first three rows. We praised and worshipped the goodness of the Lord from sunrise to sunset.

I never saw my father raise his hand or voice in praise. In fact, he was a private believer. I don't even remember seeing my father going up for prayer. He modeled his Christian life after the Good Samaritan story in the Bible. Dad lived out his faith through service. He always sat on the opposite side of the church, as a deacon did. He carried a role in the church as the patriarch of order and protection for the church members. He was always up and moving about fixing the mic or making sure the lights, heater, or AC was always working correctly.

On the other hand, I learned how to worship God by watching my mother go up in praise at the mention of the name of Jesus. She had a cute little "shout dance" in the spirit she performed as the music and praise elevated. *"I want to dance just like her when I grow up,"* I used to think to myself. She would always go up for prayer when the Pastor announced an altar call or special prayer request.

Mr. Mom

I often wondered why mom always needed special prayer. I soon found out why. My mother was very sick when I was a little girl. She was in and out of the hospital and had a hard time digesting her food. Meanwhile, my curiosity about Christ grew deeper. As a child, I wanted to have a relationship with Him as my mother did. I always thanked God for bringing my mother back home after her short hospital stays, giving God extra praise for keeping our family under his loving care and protection.

One day, she left to go to the hospital, and we didn't see her for a long time. Dad became Mr. Mom, taking care of my brother, my sister, and me. He made sure we made it to school every day with food for our bellies, fixing us a hot breakfast each morning. He packed us lunch, always putting something special in the lunch box like a note or a piece of chocolate candy. His favorite was milk chocolate peanut clusters--yum! He would brush mine and my sister's hair up in one ponytail. We sat between his long legs as he wrapped them around us to hold us in place while we wiggled from the discomfort of him pulling and tugging on our heads to make sure he got the ponytail in tight and neat.

On the weekends, he would fix us pancakes as big as a plate! He filled the black iron skillet full of pancake batter, and we would all stand around the stove to watch him masterfully flip the pancake without it splitting or breaking apart. He then would slide it into our plates, slathered it with warm butter and syrup, and tell us to go for it. He later explained that he did that, so he didn't have to stand over the stove making pancake after pancake for all of us. Four pancakes as big as a skillet, and he was done. He also loved feeling like a superhero in the kitchen while his three hungry children watched his magic.

When Mom finally returned home from the hospital, the family was always happy to be complete again. We missed her so much and couldn't wait for her to be back to her usual self. However, something had changed, and I knew it. She wouldn't tell me until almost a year later.

A Virtuous Woman

My mom, my mother, my cheerleader, my best friend, and my confidant! She learned how to manage a household under incredible personal struggles from the very beginning of her marriage. She became very depressed being away from her parents and siblings. She was extremely close to her sister Marie which brought her to tears at the thought of their childhood memories. While she was busy raising three children, all of whom were born two years apart, dad enjoyed her unconditional love for him. She lived with an expectation and her personal desire to keep Willie happy at all times, her children cared for and protected, and her family covered with the grace of God through her prayers and faithful life as a strong Christian woman.

Mom had a beautiful spirit! She loved to laugh, cook, sew, bake, watch classical movies like musicals and westerns. Most of all, she loved her children beyond any measure of love known to mankind! Mom gave life a true testament during her lifetime. She would wake us up in the mornings singing in her high, slightly off-pitched soprano voice, "Good Morning, Mary Sunshine!" I followed her around the house, stopping to observe her calm and skillful talents. Mom always taught me

19

how to manage my way around in the kitchen and the home. She cooked healthy southern-style meals because dad insisted that we would not be brought up eating what she grew up on--what he deemed unhealthy southern food. He insisted on feeding us a balance of protein, vegetables, and fiber. I would hang on to every instruction she gave me regarding how to cook, sew, wash dishes and clean up the house, help her do laundry, fold, and even iron dad's military shirts with creases in them. She even gave me instructions on watching after my sister, Esther, who was only two years younger than I. But at that time, Esther never needed any assistance from me to make her way through everyday life. She was a very independent five-year-old.

I would watch mom get up in the morning and rush to the kitchen in her robe to fix my dad a full breakfast before he left for work. The house always smelled of bacon, homemade hash browns, eggs, toast, and coffee. Pancakes and sausage were reserved for the weekend as a family treat. After dad left for work, mom worked diligently to get us ready for the day. She would cook us breakfast or let us eat our favorite cereal or pop tarts. We loved those pop tarts! Whether it was a school day or weekend, she would have our clothes ironed and laid out for us to put on. Most of the time, my sister and I dressed alike. Mom sewed most of our clothes for us. She combed our hair in the same style, and we also wore the same type of shoes. My brother always had a plaid or white short-sleeved shirt and jeans, ironed and cuffed with semi-dressy shoes. Dad would insist mom kept us looking decent whenever we left the house. After we were dressed for the day, we looked like we were either on our way to school or headed to church, even if we were just going out to play in the yard. Then mom would get herself dressed.

I admired the attention she would give herself, applying simple detail to the final outcome of her attire. She always wore a body girdle with an attached pointed bra and a slip as her undergarments. Her blouses were a solid color with three-quarter sleeves, always ironed. She would tuck her blouse into her skirt that covered her modest hips and throw on a belt to accent her waist, giving her that hourglass shape. Then she would take her bright pink sponge rollers out of her hair, popping them open and tossing them into a scarf on the bathroom counter. To my dismay, she would grab a comb and rake all the rows of curls backward, causing them to disappear in an instant. Then she'd place both her hands on both sides of her head and push her hair forward. Like magic, she had beautiful soft curls all over. To finish the transformation, she would take the comb and place it in the front and roll it forward, making the curls fall across her forehead. Then she would do the same on the sides of her head. I was in awe of her beauty. She finished by wiping her face and hands. Putting on light lip gloss while rolling her plump lips back and forth, then she was done. Unless it was a special occasion, she would not wear earrings. No makeup applied. She was done with her beauty regimen! Now it was time for her to slip on her 2" pointed-toe pumps to finish off the final touch. She always wore "nude tone" nylons or stockings. I often wondered why. I later learned that it was decent and proper for women to cover their legs; it was an expectation within our faith culture. My mother had the most beautiful legs. Her calves were muscular in shape with a sexy feminine silhouette that forced people to capture a second glance as she walked by. I know my father was captivated by her legs the day he saw her for the first time walking home in Texas.

When I was young, I loved when Mom would share her hot sweet tea with cream with me in the mornings before I left for school. After a while, I learned how to fix it for both of us. I enjoyed the fun of waiting for the teapot to whistle on the stove. Mom would pour the hot water over the teabags for us. Then, I would add just the right amount of cream and sugar to taste. I loved fixing toast and butter, which I would dip inside the teacup before savoring a bite of the delicate morsel. Oh my God, it was the best experience a daughter could have with her mother. I loved and respected her so deeply. To this day, when I drink a cup of tea, it makes me feel warm and tingly inside like I am still sharing that magical moment with Mom. We other spent precious moments together as she taught me how to sew by guiding my hand along the fabric, and showing me how to gently push the foot petal, putting her foot on top of mine. That's the way she parented—she held my hand and helped me walk through life.

Packing My First Bag

Mom always told me I was a good little girl. She smothered me with compliments and praise related to anything I did to help

22

her around the house. I was always a helper. When I was little, my dad would ask, "What do you want to be when you grow up?" I would always answer, "A teacher or a nurse." Dad would laugh. "Why a nurse?" He'd ask, then quickly follow it with, "So you can take care of me when I get old?" I would reply, "Of course, daddy but you and mom are not going to get sick or old. You and mom are gonna live forever!"

Little did I know how sick my mother was at the time and what God was preparing me for was right around the corner. I couldn't understand why Mom would break down and cry for no reason. She ate a lot of soft scrambled eggs with white bread. I noticed mom was not as active as she had been in the past. She started asking me to assist in doing more things for her while she walked around bent over, holding her stomach. She kept drinking this stuff that looked like liquid pink bubble gum in a bottle called Pepto Bismol. It looked gross! Dad would often take her to the doctor's office. Soon she wasn't eating much. She never let us know what she was going through. One day, after she returned home from the hospital, I knew something was different. Mom finally began to move around and get back to her regular routine around the house.

Months before I turned seven years old, my mom told me to come into her room because she had something to say. I began to cry but didn't let her see the tears. When I entered the room, she lay in the bed with the covers pulled up right under her breast. She told me to sit down beside her. As I did, I struggled to keep tears from swelling up in my eyes. She began to talk in a slow, comforting voice as she explained why she was in the

23

hospital for such a long time. It was because she had an operation. The doctors gave her a stoma. Then she said she wanted to show it to me on her stomach. She further explained that she had to wear a plastic bag on her stomach. I didn't understand, but I didn't want to ask any questions until she showed me what she was talking about. Then she pulled the covers down to her lower belly and revealed the plastic bag taped to her stomach.

"My intestines were not working well, so the doctors had to remove a large portion of the infected parts and only left a small amount in my stomach, but it is not enough for me to go to the bathroom like you," she said.

"Are you going to die?" I asked her. She grabbed my hand and kissed it.

"No, baby, that's why I had the operation so that I can live a long time!"

At that point, I began to cry.

"Mom, I thought you were going to tell me you were dying!". She held me close until I calmed down and my tears dried up. Then Mom showed me how she changed her colostomy bag and explained that sometimes she would need me to help her when she went to the bathroom in public. I later found out how and what I needed to do for my mother when she used a public restroom. Lastly, Mom asked me to promise her that I would not tell my brother and sister what she had shared with me. She felt my brother might not handle it well and my sister was too young. She said she would tell them when she felt the time was right. I promised her. Then, I secretly prayed to God to make my mother better so she wouldn't have another operation that would take her away from us for a long time like before. Months and months passed. At the beginning of her recovery, she continued to hold her stomach a lot. I watched my mother's every move to see if she was getting better. I did everything she asked of me and things that I thought she needed me to do without her asking. I carried the groceries for her, cleaned, and even helped her cook meals for the family. Mom never missed a beat when it came to taking care of her family. She simply adored us. Some days were better than others. It changed the course of my role as the older sister and gave me a deep appreciation as to why she had been praying and rejoicing in the Lord's mercy all those times I watched her at church. My mom lived with her stoma for 36 years. She managed her condition throughout her lifetime with grace and dignity. That incredible moment learning about my mom's stoma changed my life. I felt like I had to prepare for something more significant than the day-to-day life I had experienced thus far. A new journey was beginning to come into focus.

One day, I dreamed about packing a bag for this new journey I was preparing to take with my family. I opened my empty travel bag and placed a bible in it. I drew a heart on a piece of paper to symbolize love and compassion, then added it to my bag. I packed an encyclopedia to represent conscious reasoning and decision-making. I added a schoolbook and a nurse's hat. And, of course, I packed a large bag of French fries. Then I wrote every name of my family members on another piece of paper. I gently folded the paper so that it would last a lifetime. I kissed it, praying that God would allow me to be everything He requires me to be.

In this dream, with my bag packed, I began to travel to my secret place under a large oak tree. I looked out across a meadow of tall green grass that swayed with the wind. Then I walked towards a mountainside with huge rocks placed strategically up one side and down the other. I heard the peaceful sound of a babbling brook. I looked and noticed a fawn drinking water from it. I continued walking until I came to a valley. It started to rain, then dark clouds and lightning filled the atmosphere. Standing in that valley, I never stopped thinking about how to get back to higher ground. But there was no cover in sight. So, I had to stand in this storm until it passed.

Finally, I began to see beautiful puffy white clouds. A hawk was soaring against the breathtaking blue sky. I felt the sun warming my face. Then, I noticed a monarch butterfly perched on a blade of grass. I heard the distant sound of a small Cessna plane flying above me. At that moment, I understood why I existed in this world. I grabbed my bag, prepared to live out my predestined role as a caretaker and loving member of my family. Then I woke up. I knew there would be times in life where I'd find myself in a dark valley, facing a storm. Mom taught me to never stop looking for higher ground, even if I have to endure a storm. It was time to continue my journey in real life.

OUR FAMILY

First-Born Only Brother

L ife in the McGee family was something to behold. We were the perfect example of a family that loved unconditionally. My older brother, Edwin Leroy, known to us as Leroy, was quiet and reserved even at a young age. He always found fun things to do outside and wanted me to be his right-hand partner in doing so. He was adventurous, never allowing anything to hold him back from taking on a personal quest to challenge his boyhood. My parents told me that when we were toddlers in Hawaii, I would pull him around all day in his red wagon. He would sit quietly and motion *Lol* towards the direction he wanted to go with a simple point of his finger. Without question, I would turn and reverse that wagon until I knew he was pleased with my navigation. As a young child, Leroy used his intelligence in clever ways that kept my parents laughing to the point of drawing tears! He loved apples. One day, he wanted another apple. However, when he asked for another one, my dad told him "no." Knowing that when dad said no, he meant no, and there was no need for further discussion, Leroy decided if he couldn't see my parents, then, of course, they couldn't see him. So, he closed his eyes and scaled the living room wall until he reached the kitchen wall. Then, eyes still closed, Leroy scaled across the kitchen wall until he made it to the refrigerator. With his eyes closed, he felt around for the refrigerator door handle and opened it. His hand patted around until it reached the fruit bin, then he pulled out a delicious red apple. He took a big bite out of it, then slowly made his way past my parents with his eyes closed until he made it to the stairs with the half-eaten apple. Dad didn't have the heart to discipline him at the moment, but the next time Leroy asked for an apple, he knew how my dad felt about his past actions. My brother never tried that trick again.

As children, my brother and I would play outside all day together. I would love to go on some of his "you know we shouldn't" adventures. We would get in trouble for being too far away from the house. When we returned, we would always make sure it was both our fault and never blamed the other. I had no problem being a little tomboy. Leroy taught me how to play marbles. I was so happy when I finally learned how to make them skip. He also taught me how to use a yo-yo, throw a knuckleball, hit a baseball, play with cars and dump trucks, play in creeks, challenge him in races, and climb trees. Sometimes I think he would forget that I was a little girl and some things like climbing trees in a dress weren't very appropriate! I taught

Leroy some things, such as playing jacks, jump rope, hula hoop, and hopscotch--none of which he enjoyed playing with me.

My brother taught me how to fight and defend myself when I was bullied or picked on at school. We never left each other's side when we played together outside in our neighborhood. It wasn't safe to do so being the only children of color. My parents always told us to stay together; to this day, we are inseparable! During our younger years, my brother always made me feel important. He would make sure I did the things that would please mom and dad, such as doing well in school. He would tell me not to get in trouble and not to fight. He would proudly let everyone know I was his younger sister. That added an extra layer of protection for me. We always walked or rode the bus to school together. All through elementary school, I felt my brother was my protector. We were two years apart at the same school, so I often saw him during lunch. I would give him my peanut butter and jelly sandwich even if he didn't ask for it. Sometimes Dad would treat us to McDonald's. I LOVED McDonald's French fries!! As a kid, I would savor every hot, salty, crispy fry, enjoying the rich starchy flavor. First, I would gently slide them past my lips, across the sensors of my taste buds, pushing them back to my molars as I moved them side to side while chewing. I'd dare myself not to swallow, just so I could savor the moment. Then with anticipation of the next mouth-watering sensation, I'd reach into the bag to start that experience all over again. At the same time, out of the corner of my eyes, I'd watch my brother scarf his bag of fries and then look my way to see if I had any left. Without thinking twice, I would give him my last few fries. That is how much childhood love I had for my brother. My love has matured now; my fries are my prized possession--I don't share. I don't have a problem buying him some, though.

As for me, Leroy is my HERO! He is simply amazing! He moves with confidence and lives making every moment of his life purposeful. He does whatever he wants to do. He speaks his truth, challenges his aspirations, and questions the unknown. Leroy is a daredevil. Unlike the rest of us McGee siblings, he seeks happiness in ways that may be too risky for others.

Leroy has a charming smile, just like my dad. His sense of humor is off the cuff, cynical, and at times, jaw-dropping. I learned over the years not to take it personally because he is the most loving brother that a sister could ever dream of, pray for, and want. He is a protective, strong, alpha male without any second thoughts of letting you know it. He is athletic with an attractive muscular build. He carries himself in a manner of charm and captures a compliment for his presence wherever he goes.

First Sister

My sister Esther is my most independent, self-focused, theatrical-minded sibling. She is a confident person. Esther can walk into a room full of people who have credentials and life experience far above hers and then challenge each of their intellects. She knew she would reign superior when it was all said and done. Her beauty is stunning! Her long jet-black hair, voluptuous body frame, and legs that matched my mom's shape and size always got her a thumbs up when compared to any female. As children growing up together, Esther seemed to be an intrigued observer of my role as her older sister. I've always thought of her as a secret thinker and a bold doer; she wanted to be one who accomplished everything first. We spent incredible moments of our childhood enhancing our innate creative ability to think and do things that were mature for our age. Those were some of our best years growing up together.

Esther always paved her own path. Even as a young child, she had her own opinion on how she wanted to live in the image of being a McGee. She seems to be at her best when she is in her own lane, marching to the beat of her own drum. I struggled throughout our growing up together to convince Esther to accept that I was her older sister. In public, she often told people she was the oldest sibling whenever it was in question. I would just laugh it off, but when we got older, I started to welcome being referred to as the younger sister. I considered it as a compliment.

When we were living in Oklahoma City, I told Esther I would take her on a picnic. We made saltine peanut butter crackers and packed them in a small brown paper bag. I was so proud that she was going to ride on the seat of my bike. I prepared to pedal her up the hill to the park around the corner from our house. As we were balancing ourselves on the bike next to the curb, trying to get enough courage to take off without falling, something strange was happening. Esther and I could not stop laughing because we would lose our balance every time we started to take off. We must have been on that curbside for a long time. When I looked down at the bike pedal, I noticed we were standing on a vast red ant hill. The ants had begun crawling up our legs and biting us. We were so consumed with laughing and joking about falling, we hadn't noticed. We both immediately hopped off the bike and jumped up and down, beating off the ants while screaming and crying for mom. We ran into the house, and immediately mother ran a tub of bath water and told us to jump in. As the ants were falling off our bodies and floating in the water, I felt terrible that I didn't notice the anthill. I felt worse to see that my little sister had ant bites because of my grand idea of going on a picnic. I really wanted to do something fun with her, and it turned out to be a disaster. To this day, I am bug phobic, and yet we still laugh together about that experience. We did eat the peanut butter crackers later. Some of our favorite play time was spent dressing up paper dolls. We would play together with them for hours.

Miracle from God

Soon I noticed that mom wasn't taking the Pepto Bismol anymore, which made me assume she was getting better. As I counted down the days to my 7th birthday in April, I was looking forward to a homemade birthday cake with lots of frosting! I started to notice that mom's tummy was growing in size. I knew our family was about to add one more addition! We never talked about it in detail. Then, mom asked me to come to her bedroom for a second time because she had something to tell me. I was prepared to hear that I would be a big sister again because she was having a baby. When she did, I jumped up and down with joy. I was too young to even imagine or consider what she must have endured being pregnant with a stoma and so soon after her surgery. One day, out of the blue, Dad told us he was taking mom to the hospital to have a baby and that she would be there for a while. I thought for a moment that God hadn't heard the prayer I prayed when she told me about her stoma because she was leaving our family again. I was so scared. Mom had to have a cesarean delivery due to her stoma. It was a risky pregnancy and delivery. Years later, she shared with me that she could have died going through with her pregnancy. Dad was afraid of losing mom, but the doctor told dad that because of her deep depression she was experiencing due to having her stoma, having my sister would be the best thing for her. It would give her a reason to live past her severe bouts of depression. After a month or so, my father told us to get dressed and took us to the military hospital to meet our new sibling. My brother was nine, my sister was five. My 7th birthday had passed a few weeks prior, without that homemade cake with lots of frosting.

We all sat in a cold, brick-walled waiting room in anticipation. Finally, I saw my dad pushing mom down the hallway with her bundle of joy tightly wrapped in a pink blanket. Mom slowly made a weak smile as she approached the reception of us waving and clapping our hands in excitement. I could tell she wasn't feeling well, as her smile quickly dissipated after acknowledging us. As dad got closer, he secured the wheelchair brakes. He gestured to the bundle of joy as he announced in a serious tone,

"This is Baby Sister.³" Then he lifted my sister out of my mother's arms, walked over to me, and placed her in my arms. He looked directly into my eyes and said, "Your mother is too weak to take care of her. You are going to be responsible for taking care of Baby Sister until your mother feels stronger." I looked over at my mom, and she gave me a wink and a nod. Then, in a low but comforting voice, "I know you can do it because you're her big sister, and you always help mommy out with everything. I will teach you and help you do as much as I can." I looked down at Baby Sister. She looked like a tiny doll! She had jet-black hair that was so thick and curly! She had large, dreamy eyes like my father and matching deep dimples just like my mom. Her skin was a creamy porcelain hue. Her warm newborn body radiating from the blanket felt like I was holding a true miracle sent to us by God. My siblings gathered around her and made their presence known. They were in awe of her existence.

I stood there in shock and fear, not wanting to disappoint my parents in carrying out the role I was just assigned. I didn't know whether to hand her back to my mom, give her to dad, or allow my brother and sister to take her from me. They were both reaching out to get their turn to hold her. Dad rescued me from my inner dilemma and scooped Baby Sister from my shaking arms. He placed her in Mom's lap and released the brakes from her wheelchair, and we all walked together toward the exit door. It seemed as if the whole world suddenly became

Out of respect for my youngest sister's privacy, I have not included her name in this book. She is referred to throughout as "Baby Sister."

still and strangely silent. I was in my own head about what just happened. I wanted to know if my mother would be ok and why she was too weak to take care of her child. I predicted that mom would probably be calling me back into her room to tell me the reason why. But for the moment, I let it all go out of my head. I was just happy that our beautiful family was together again. At seven years old, it was the best feeling ever!

Mother taught me everything I needed to know to care for Baby Sister--how to change and clean cloth diapers, fix her bottles, bathe and dress her. I played and read to her, sang songs, and rocked her to sleep every night. She wouldn't sleep unless she was next to someone. We spoiled her and loved every minute of it. I was delighted to know my mother could trust me to do everything for my sister as she rested and allowed her body to heal. Baby Sister was a miracle sent from God. She was such a beautiful little baby. Caring for her made me feel like I was the luckiest sister on earth. We were settling into a routine now that our family was complete.

"No more children," dad would say. "Four hungry mouths to feed are more than enough."

Baby Sister had two mommies, including me; she took full advantage of it. She never lacked anything. All of us catered to her every need and made sure she was happy and content as she could be. Baby Sister brought joy to all of us and gave us one more reason to appreciate the blessing of being a McGee!

I had a beautiful relationship with Baby Sister growing up. We were everything to each other. She was my prized possession, and I was her role model. I did all I could to teach her all the things mom taught and showed me. She is beautiful like Esther, but shy to draw public attention. As a child, she was curious about life, always thinking and questioning anything that didn't match how she processed life. She gave me such a challenge trying to keep her happy, especially during her temper tantrums. She asked complicated and intriguing questions; she never accepted 'I don't know" for an answer. I always had to come up with a solution that satisfied her. Then she would come up with another question for me to answer. I was her protector. I never wanted anything to hurt or harm her in any way. She always wanted to be with me and go everywhere I went.

Baby Sister carried a mysterious intellect about herself. She always loved putting things together and figuring out how to do things differently than what was expected. Dad always considered her the smartest of all his children and never hesitated to say so. She captured his heart as the one who would most follow his professional pathway because of her intellect. All of us gave Baby Sister that platform because none of us desired to follow dad in that manner. Leroy was following the path of an athlete; Esther and I were humanitarians at best. At the time, Baby Sister was too young to know the difference, so dad graciously took advantage of determining it for her. Only time would tell what path all of us would untimely take in life.

The McGee siblings marched to the beat of dad's drum. When he wasn't there, we danced to the music of my mom's heart. Dad set the rules. Mom always found a way to bend them in our favor. I always questioned the rules, Leroy challenged them, and Esther made her own. Baby Sister, being the youngest, was fortunate to have fewer rules to follow.

There it is. I always felt that

Discipline
Tere in CB

During my childhood years, we grew incredibly close as a family. Dad and Mom kept us near and dear to them. Their rule of thumb was that they were solely responsible for their children. No one else could ever fit the bill of raising us the way they wanted us raised. Also, as their children, we were responsible for the care and protection of each other. *What is*

We had to constantly look decent in our dress, speak in proper English, protect and respect one another, keep a clean room and a clean house inside and out. He expected mom to always have vegetables on our dinner plates. Every evening when we gathered around the dinner table, dad would say grace, and all of us properly consumed our food under his rule about table manners. I looked forward to the conversations we had as a family at dinner time. We ate dinner together every night and breakfast together on most weekends. *American Anglo Dream*

Weekends were inspection days. Dad would call for random room inspections and expect our beds to be made military-style, with the sheets tucked at the ends in a triangle and tight as a snare drum. He would literally attempt to bounce a quarter off them. Then he would put his white gloves on and run his fingers across our dressers and the top of the door. Our clothes had to be ironed and hung up.

It weird. is
this but
how good
cause
damage

Dad would not allow us to sleep in on the weekends. He would yell, "GET UP AND BE PRODUCTIVE!" We had to figure out what measured up to his productive standard. We couldn't sit and watch TV for an extended amount of time before he would tell us to turn it off and get a book to read. He didn't care what we read. We just had to read something, the bible, a magazine, a schoolbook--it didn't matter! We weren't allowed to raise our voices at each other. Dad always wanted a low volume of noise in the house. He wouldn't tolerate our voices competing with the television. We couldn't do our homework with the TV or radio on. It had to be reasonably quiet in the house so that we could concentrate. We weren't allowed to come home without schoolbooks. Dad expected homework every day. The dishes had to be sparkling clean. For example, if one of us missed a dirty spot on a glass, he would put every glass back into the sink to be rewashed.

Rules in the McGee household were strictly enforced. Dad's disciplinary style was punitive and sometimes unforgiving. He followed a military-style regiment of expected behavior and gave it to us straight. Dad firmly believed in corporal punishment and never hesitated in making the decision to spank us when we fell out of line. Mom gave her gentle disapproval in a permissive way when she felt he was too hard on us.

Taking A Licking

One Sunday, Leroy, Esther, and I were in church cutting up, talking, and laughing together. Dad gave us one long look of disapproval and waved his pointer finger at us. We immediately knew we were in trouble. On the way home from church, he told us we were completely out of order to be talking during the service and that all of us were going to get a spanking. Mother defended by telling dad that we were just kids and doing what kids do. She even tried to convince dad that spanking us wasn't necessary. We tried begging for forgiveness and talking our way out of it, but none of it worked.

When we arrived home, Leroy said to Esther and me, "Hurry up, go in the room, and put as many pairs of underwear on as you can so it won't hurt when he spanks us." Dad spanked us with a belt instead of his hand so he wouldn't have known our butts were padded. As we waddled out of our rooms like little ducklings with padded butts, he added, "Cry really loud and hard. It will make him stop after a few licks."

We all lined up outside mom and dad's bedroom. Leroy went in first. After the first lick, Leroy screamed out painfully. As dad continued, he got louder and louder. Dad stopped after about four licks. Leroy came out smiling at us. Then it was my time. Once dad hit me, I tried to outdo Leroy. I screamed in agonizing pain. Dad stopped after about two or three licks. Leroy gave me a high five when I came out and told me I did a good job. Then it was Esther, the drama queen's turn. Before she even got through the door, she started screaming at the top of her lungs, pleading and begging dad not to spank her. She yelled and cried, hollered, and gasped for air. We could hear her feet dancing around on the wooden floor. Then we heard maybe half a lick of the belt hitting her butt. Then silence. The door opened, and she came out with the biggest grin on her face without a tear in her eyes. She got the Academy Award for best performance and no spanking! That was my sister for you!

Forgiveness

Esther and I once got into a physical shuffle over a hairbrush when she was 10 and I was 12 years old. When dad found out, he pulled every clean dish out of the cupboards and told us to rewash all of them together! If he found that they weren't thoroughly washed, dried, and put away, we would get our butts beaten. We were so angry at each other, but we knew we had to get the job done and get it right. When we finished, I was so saddened by the incident; I knew that Dad had taught us to treat each other better. So, I wrote Esther a letter that read:

Dear Esther, I do not want this. I want to be lovely sisters and love each other and not fight. Esther, I really do love you, and I hope you love me too. It always seems that I am always the one to make up first, but it is because I want to be forgiven by you only. I am very sorry. I love you, Cynthia. Do you forgive me? YES OR NO? _____

She returned the same note to me, crossing out her name in the greeting and adding mine. She crossed out the word "first" and changed it to "last" and told me she loved me too.

"PS. "I am a sorehead," she added.

That was the first and only time we had a physical shuffle. I still have that letter to this day!

ESTHER'S APOLOGY

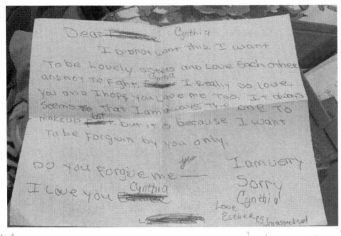

Dear ~~Esther~~ Cynthia
I did not want this, I want
To be lovely sisters and love each other
and not to fight. ~~Cynthia~~ I really do love
you and I hope you love me too. It always
Seems ~~to~~ that I am always the one to
makeups ~~lost~~ but it is because I want
To be forgiven by you only.

Do you forgive me yes I am very
I love you ~~Cynthia~~ Sorry
Cynthia
~~Esther~~ Love,
Esther P.S I'm a sorehead

Made me realize just how horrible
our/my life was

One day, Mom asked me to go to the store to get some milk
and eggs. Of course, Baby Sister wanted to go, and mom told
me to take her with me. Although I knew I could get there and
back faster without dragging her along, I couldn't hurt her
feelings by leaving her behind. She loved to carry the money,
so I let her do so. When we arrived at the store, she immediately
began to ask for some candy. I told her no because I knew mom
had not given me permission to get any. After paying for the
groceries, she asked again, and I repeated no. Then I handed
her the change hoping this would keep her happy until we got
home. Immediately she threw all the change across the floor in
the store, in anger! I yelled at her for doing that and said, "I'm
going to tell dad when we got back home." I crawled around
on the floor, picked up the money, and counted it to make sure
it was all there. Then I grabbed her by the hand and couldn't
wait to get home to tell dad how much she embarrassed me.

Why?

She begged me not to tell, but I really wanted her to know that she cannot be disrespecting me like that in public.

As soon as we stepped into the door of our house, she started crying and saying that she was sorry. At that point, my heart softened. I quickly made up my mind not to tell dad what happened. However, he heard the commotion and asked me what happened and why Baby Sister was crying. I had to tell him the truth. Dad chastised her. He then told her she was getting a spanking and began to take off his belt.

"Dad, stop!" I yelled. "She apologized, and I forgave her!"

It didn't matter. As he moved toward her, I jumped in and tried to grab the belt. After two licks, he stopped because I was yelling and crying right along with her. Dad simply shook his head and walked away from both of us, standing in the room consoling each other.

When I got my first babysitting job, I bought Baby Sister her first black baby doll named DeBe. It made Baby Sister so happy, and she treasured it. She carried that doll around, even after the body had fallen off. I'm pretty sure she still has that doll head today. Baby Sister always wrote me cute little notes expressing her genuine love for me.

LETTERS FROM BABY SISTER THAT I'VE KEPT OVER THE YEARS

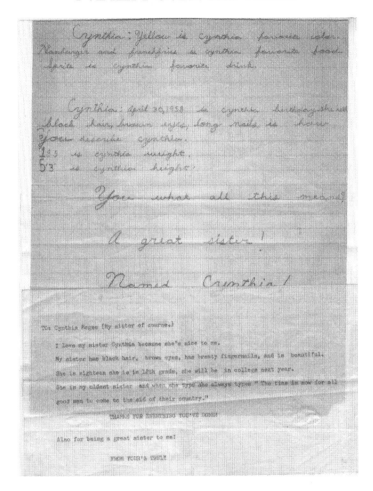

Man to Man

Leroy was about sixteen years old when he got in trouble for talking back to dad. During this time of his life, he was playing sports and working out every day. His body was developing muscles he didn't even know he had, so he felt pretty cocky!

43

Dad ripped his belt off of his waist and proceeded to approach Leroy with his arm raised high in the air. Leroy grabbed dad's arm and moved it away from him. Then he jumped up like Bruce Lee, did a high kick in the air, and landed in the best-formed karate fighting stance I've ever seen. Dad took a confused look at him and said, "I guess you are getting too old for me to spank you." Then Dad walked away. I laughed and cheered Leroy's show of courage to challenge dad.

"What were you going to do next if Dad hadn't walked away?" I asked.

"I don't know. All I know is that I didn't want to get hit with that belt," he said.

As we got older, dad began to have talks and discussions with us when he felt we needed to be redirected or disciplined. He would sit us down at the kitchen table to talk about his expectations and consequences. His rules were still strict. Sometimes it was hard for me to accept them without challenging him. He said if I had a problem with them, come to him with a solution in mind. Otherwise, it was not to be discussed, and the rule would stand. Dad's lesson on how to challenge rules is safely packed in my bag of life essentials.

Actions Speak Louder Than Words

Our mom was totally different in her disciplinary style. She favored a more emotional response to our misbehavior. Her shaming hurt worse than the spankings dad gave us. She would yell at the top of her voice when we misbehaved. She never wanted to spank us. She just yelled, using her emotional swats across our hearts to correct any behavior. One time I was upset at mom for a childish reason. Everyone was getting their hair pressed and curled. Mom did my hair last. My sisters had long, thick hair; my hair was short and wispy. But that day, my ponytail seemed longer to me, so I showed it off to Mom. When she didn't respond with any praise or the acknowledgment I wanted, I felt chicken-headed compared to my sisters. But mom was busy and just went on to the next thing. Since I felt ignored, I decided not to talk to mom for the rest of the day. She noticed my behavior but never said a word to me about it.

The next day was her shopping day at the navy base commissary. I always went with her, so as she was preparing to go, so was I.

"When are we leaving?" I asked her. She didn't answer me.

An hour later, she headed out the door toward the parking lot. I ran to my bedroom window, which faced the parking lot. "Are you going to the commissary?" I yelled.

She simply shook her head yes. "Can I go with you?" I asked. She shook her head no. She didn't look back and didn't say a word to me. As she walked to her car, I yelled her name louder and louder until she got in and drove off. I fell breathlessly on my bed and literally cried the whole time she was gone.

When she came back, she came directly into my room and said, "Never treat me like you did, Cynthia. It was disrespectful and hurtful."

When I explained why I was ignoring her, she said, "You should have told me. Now we both know how it feels to be ignored by someone you love." It was a powerful lesson on the value of communication.

Oh wow, I did that to you

For the Love of Food

Dad was very concerned about our health, along with our shape and size. He was tough on me as his first daughter. He tried to make me the example of his preferred image of a young, growing girl. He had a critical eye when it came to the female physique and was concerned that I would become overweight. He told my mom when I was around eight years old that I was getting fat. Dad insisted that she put me on a diet. I was devastated. Not because he thought I was fat, but because it meant that I couldn't do what I loved doing the most, which was eating. I remember dad and mom getting into discussions about my weight and what type of diet I should be on. It was decided that I should eat salad, tuna, and crackers. It felt like that was all I ate forever. My mother would help me cheat on the diet by sneaking me "forbidden foods" before dad came home from work. She even ate tuna and salad with me to make me feel better.

As I was nearing the end of my diet regimen, my mom baked a white cake with buttercream frosting. It smelled delicious! I remember praying that dad would let me have some cake after dinner. However, I also thought just in case he wouldn't, I needed to make sure I got a taste on my own. The cake sat on the table under the window in the dining room. I needed to come up with a way to taste the frosting, if nothing else. So, I decided to play an imaginary game with the blinds on the window next to the cake, addressing them as "Mr. Blinds." While mom was tending to other chores in the house, I knew it was only a matter of time before dad came home from work. With my mouth watering for the taste of the buttercream frosting, I crawled under the table to the cake which faced the wall under the window. I reached up and pulled on the string of the blinds.

"Mr. Blinds, could I please have a taste of the frosting?" I asked. Then I opened up the blinds to indicate his answer, "Yes, of course!"

With a deep swipe into the cake base, I scooped up frosting with my finger and quickly licked it off. It was delicious, just as I had imagined it would be.

Now my taste buds were fully awakened, and my greed was too. I looked around and listened for mom's footsteps. When it was all clear, I quickly closed the blinds and pulled on the string again, asking for permission to taste the frosting. As I opened the blinds, I complimented Mr. Blinds for being so kind and saying yes. However, this time I took an even bigger scoop of frosting using two fingers. That frosting slid down my throat, giving me the most pleasurable moment of sweetness. I think I slipped into a sugar-induced state of unconsciousness. I didn't hear or see my mom standing over me until she began to laugh uncontrollably.

"Cynthia!" she called, "What in the world are you doing under the table? And what happened to the frosting on my cake?" As I crawled from under the table, I knew I was in trouble. She asked me again. I told her how much I wanted some cake and thought dad wasn't going to let me have a slice after dinner. So, I made up a game with the blinds to get permission to taste it. She continued to laugh at me as she went into the kitchen to get a knife to redistribute the frosting over the areas that I had swiped my fingers through. She promised me she wouldn't tell dad. "Next time, just ask for some cake. I would have made sure you got a slice." Her gentle chastisement was endearing. That was just the way she was. I loved her for it.

While living in Oklahoma, our family was invited over to our Pastor's house for Sunday dinner. Dad had reminded us of our table manners before we arrived. They grew all their own vegetables in their backyard garden. It was the first time I tasted fresh green beans with potatoes. I enjoyed them so much I didn't think twice before I asked, without permission from my parents, to have a second helping. The look on my dad's face as he turned to catch my eyes across the table was as if he had just come face to face with his worst enemy.

"No, she is fine," Dad said, before the Pastor's wife could answer.

Our Pastor and his wife went back and forth with dad, trying to convince dad to change his mind.

"They are vegetables," they said. "It's great to see a child love them enough to ask for more."

Nevertheless, when we got home, I was lectured for an hour on how rude it was for me to ask for seconds on anything.

"You never know how much food a family has and how much they stretched their money and resources to feed our family of six," my dad admonished me.

I had never thought about it that way. I thought all they had to do was go out to the backyard and pick more green beans instead of buying them at the store. To this day, I always overcook when I prepare meals. If someone wants a second serving of food at my table, I never want them to feel the way I did that day. I love to eat. Food is where I go when I want to celebrate happiness, accomplish a goal, or even when I have fallen short of one. I admit eating and cooking food is my happy place in life.

A Relationship with God

My parents' teaching to be considerate of others replaced most temptation to consider myself first. However, my selflessness became one of the gifts I have given away repeatedly throughout my life as an abundant return on the investment my parents made in me. It's essential to identify the gifts you were given or blessed with. Once you do, look for opportunities to give them away over and over again. In doing so, blessings will come your way. It was the biblical and spiritual teachings of my parents--love thy neighbor, charity starts at home, do unto others. Those Christian intentions were instilled in me.

My personal relationship with God began when I was just seven years old in a small tent outdoor revival at our church when we lived in Oklahoma City. We attended the revival every day for almost a week. I was around eight years old. At the time, I thought I was too young to have the same spiritual experience as the adults. But I really wanted to. People would kneel at the altar for hours to do what they called "tarrying for the Holy Spirit." As a child, this tarrying for the Holy Spirit seemed to be a difficult thing to accomplish. Everyone who went to the altar said "Thank You Jesus" over and over, only stopping to catch a breath or swallow. This would go on until they received the Holy Spirit by speaking in tongues. However, sometimes this process would cause a build-up of saliva in the mouth due to their throat drying. I guess taking a drink of water was prohibited and would interfere with the process. It was all so strange to me, but I wanted to feel whatever everyone else was feeling and experiencing.

So one day, I boldly went to the altar and kneeled down to begin my chant of "Thank You, Jesus!" After a few minutes, I began to look around. I noticed some of the members had that saliva buildup around their mouths. I knew that once that happened, the Holy Spirit was near. So, I closed my eyes tight and started yelling, "Thank You, Jesus," as loud as I could. Nothing happened. So, I decided to help the Holy Spirit by spitting as much saliva out of my mouth as possible. Before I knew it, I was snatched up by the collar of my blouse, nearly suspended in the air for a few seconds, and then spanked all the way to the inside bathroom of the church.

When I came to my senses and my vision returned to focus, I saw Sister Beavers, Baby Sister's Godmother. She was the head deaconess of the church, standing in front of me with her hands on her wide hips. She stared past my face and into my soul, with the meanest look of disgust for what I did. With her stern voice, she scolded me with deep conviction about what I did at the altar.

"Why would you do such a thing?" she asked me.

"I really wanted the Holy Spirit like everyone else," I told her.

With a stern voice, she replied, "The Holy Spirit doesn't need to be forced. First, all you have to do is ask him to forgive you for your sins so you can be saved. He will hear your request and enter into your heart. That is where he wants to feel your love for Him. Stop trying to do what everyone else is doing. God wants you to be in your own special relationship with Him."

The next day we went back to the revival. I sat in my chair in that tent, determined not to do anything wrong. The choir began to sing a song called *"Pass Me Not Oh Gentle Savior."* It was a slow song with a gentle plea for salvation. I still hear the saints of old singing, Her Altar call

"Savior, Savior hear my humble cry, while all others thou art calling do not pass me by."

As I listened to the words and the beautiful melody being played on the piano, I simply began to cry. The warmest feeling came over me as I started singing the lyrics of the song. My hands went up in reverence to God, and my heart began to beat in rhythm with the words of the song. I prayed for forgiveness of my sins and picked up singing the chorus of the song,

"Do not pass me by!"

That day, He didn't. I felt his presence not only in my heart but all throughout my being. It was the best feeling in the world. I learned that when I am in my own space and place of being and believing in what I know is and feels right, heaven opens up, and the stars align. The angels sing, and my relationship with God allows me to be centered in his will. In God's will is where I feel safest and most secure in living my life. Being complete in my relationship with God hasn't always been full of bliss and sweet-smelling roses.

Life challenges threw me a curveball or two during my journey. I work hard to stay focused on what helps me to be at my best in any circumstance. However, I keep my bag packed full of spiritual conviction and biblical principles. These are the essentials I never unpack. They are like my emergency kit, my lifeline, my oxygen, my love that never dissipates. My parents taught us the value of unconditional love, and God showed me what it looks like and feels like. That double dose of love is incredible. Our family practiced always trying to be at our best self with one another. Mom and Dad held us accountable for showing one another love.

In the early stages of my life, we took both short trips and long travels together as my dad was relocated by the Air Force. However, as we grew older, short trips and long travels merged into one continuous journey while searching for our individual destinies. It became clear how this took shape as time accumulated into years. Wisdom became the compass, and our life experiences became the vehicle of change.

TRIPS AND TRAVELS

Life's A Trip; Pack A Bag

Dad's assignments took us from coast to coast during his more than twenty-two years of service in the United States Air Force. After leaving Hawaii in 1960, we were stationed in Oklahoma City. We stayed there for almost four years. In 1964, we moved from Oklahoma City to Niagara Falls, New York, where we lived for two years. We were then stationed in Montana, spending one year in Glasgow and another year in Opheim. In 1968, we returned to Midwest City, Oklahoma, for almost two years. Dad was stationed in Alaska for one of those years. In 1969, we were stationed in Morro Bay, California, for two years. Finally, in 1971 when I was 12 years old, my family was stationed in El Cajon, California, where we settled until dad retired.

It was complicated moving so much, but it was a lot of fun when dad got new orders. We would travel in a station wagon across the country together. That is the only type of car dad would buy. He said we were a big family, and we needed room to grow. Every time Dad got orders, he would come home and tell us with such excitement. He loved having the opportunity to see another part of the country. Then he would sit us around the table and spread the US road map open before us. Dad would map out our course and then highlight the sightseeing places along the way, giving special attention to the national parks and areas like Mount Rushmore and the Petrified Forest. It was always an adventure! After Dad excited us about the trip to our next destination, the hard work of moving and packing up our home would begin. It was a huge ordeal for us. As children, we hardly wanted to focus on getting things ready for the movers to come. Dad always made it easier on the movers. He wanted everything organized and some items pre-wrapped and labeled so when it arrived at our new home, he would know exactly where to look for it. I could hardly wait for the large yellow and green Mayflower moving truck to pull up next to our house. When it did, I knew the next day we would be leaving to go on our long journey in our green station wagon. Those family road trips held some of my best childhood memories of us being together as a family. I loved falling to sleep with the sound of the car tires rolling along on the highway and the soft swaying motion the big semi-trucks would cause as they passed us in the middle of the night. I could hear mom and dad strategizing about a safe motel stay in the next town. Dad would always go in to check it out first. If it did not meet his approval, he would get back in the car and drive, all night if necessary, until he reached the next town and could check us into a motel of his liking. I didn't mind the extended travel time in the car. I just loved sleeping in the back, sandwiched between all my siblings, listening to the sounds of the car engine along with the whistling wind. The blinking lights of the cities we passed through flashed outside the window as the jazz music's soothing sound played on the radio. We were on our way to New York.

Niagara Falls

Once we settled into base housing in Niagara Falls, New York, I felt it was different from our life in Oklahoma City. There weren't any creeks in the back of the house. I didn't see any vegetable gardens either. Even the church was different. The church we attended was in Buffalo City, New York. People dressed in fancy attire with big hats that covered nearly their whole face. My parents always wanted us to attend church to give us a cultural experience. However, it was short-lived in Buffalo. One day, I remember going to church and hearing loud screaming and cussing between two ladies as we entered the building. Dad moved us along but not fast enough before they began to push and shove each other. It quickly turned into a fight! They slapped and shoved, pulled, and ripped off each other's hats and wigs. My mother was trying to get us to a safe place while dad tried to separate them.

When everything had calmed down, Dad said to the Pastor, "This will be the last time my family will attend your church. I will not have my wife and children put in harm's way while trying to serve God. This is not what I want to be the example

57

of Christian living." My family talked about it all the way home. It was the first time I had seen Black people fight each other. I always thought we were supposed to fight with White people. I didn't understand how Black people could hurt each other the same way White people hurt us. I was saddened by the reality. I still struggle to understand it to this day.

Living in Niagara Falls was a fun experience. Dad always tried to expand our life experiences past living in our small, protected world. We were sightseeing all over. I loved going to see Niagara Falls. The view was scary and breathtaking at the same time. We saw the Statue of Liberty and Times Square. One day, he drove us back to Buffalo City to let us see how other people lived. These people were not as fortunate as my siblings and me, who were living as military brats. I learned that we were blessed to live on-base, away from some of the challenges peers in less fortunate communities faced. I never forgot the images of the broken-down homes and buildings on streets covered with trash. Dad vowed never to have his family live in such conditions.

At the time, I felt that being a Black girl in a predominantly White community made me a target for ridicule and mockery. One day, it was raining hard. I was preparing to catch the school bus and was running late. Mom handed me my umbrella as I ran out the door as the bus was waiting. I picked up my speed while opening the umbrella. Sadly, my weak little umbrella couldn't withstand the wind and hard rain. It flipped inside out. I continued to run in hopes that the bus would continue to wait for me. I was getting soaked but thought it was because the storm was worsening. As I got closer to the bus, I noticed all the children pointing and laughing at me. I became distraught. I almost wished the driver would take off and leave me so I wouldn't have to face everyone once I got on the bus. But the driver didn't. As I approached the doors, I reached up to close my umbrella. All the water in my flipped umbrella came splashing down onto my head, drenching me! The children on the bus laughed louder. I even noticed the bus driver was laughing. Then someone said, "We were trying to let you know your umbrella was broken, but you wouldn't look up!"

I realized they hadn't been laughing at me for being a little Black girl who was about to miss the school bus. Instead, maybe they were trying to help me. I exhaled a sigh of relief. Then accepted how funny I must have looked to everyone, and I joined in on the laughter. We laughed about the incident for the rest of the ride to school. When I got home, I shared the story with my mom. She told me she had seen the whole thing and was also yelling my name, trying to let me know the umbrella was broken, and that she too had been laughing at me. She said it was a funny sight to see! Humor is good for the soul, and I love to laugh. That day brings a smile to my face every time I think about it. Dad soon got orders to relocate to Montana.

Brownie

In 1966, we moved from Niagara Falls to Montana. We moved to Glasgow first, but it was too far of a drive to the military base in Opheim. After six months, we moved to base housing in Opheim.

I always played "school" at home. I created an inclusive, make-believe school for all my dolls and stuffed animals. Sometimes other neighborhood kids would humor me by volunteering as students in my classroom.

No matter what, I always had one committed student who was the smartest and never missed a day in my class. It was Baby Sister. She would always play school with me. I never knew if she truly loved it or if she just didn't know how to ask me for a pass out of class or school for the day. My sister Esther would play with me, but I had to share the teaching role with her. I didn't like giving up the title because I was the oldest, and teachers were supposed to be older than their students! Mom played a role by letting me fix snacks that I used for lunchtime. Everyone got a lunch, even if the dolls and stuffed animals couldn't eat it. I would eat it all for them--delicious!

I was growing up and looking for other ways to be the social butterfly. While I was sitting in my cold classroom in Opheim one day, my teacher passed out an application to become a Brownie Scout. As the teacher explained all the activities and adventures associated with the Brownie Scouts, I became very excited. I couldn't wait to get home to ask my parents if I could join. I ran off the bus holding the application with the tightest grip possible. The cold wind chilled my face as I sped to the house, trying to beat the time it usually took me to arrive home from school. I left my brother at the bus stop. He had no reason

Im learning so much about you CB

to rush home. I was jumping over piles of snow. When I opened the door, I could hardly catch my breath.

"Mom, can I become a Brownie, pleeeeease?" I begged.

Mom said she already knew about the Scouts. She was considering applying to become a troop leader and was excited that I was interested in joining. But she told me I had to ask dad.

I waited on pins and needles until Dad came home from work. I didn't even want him to take off his hat and settle down before I popped the question.

"Dad, can I become a Brownie?" I waved the application back and forth across his chest as he stood over me. He took the paper and glanced at it. Then he replied, "You are already a Brownie."

I didn't get it at first; I was only listening for the "No." But, after a few moments, I understood.

"Oh, you mean my skin color, huh, dad?"

"Yup," he replied. *I never finish anything*

That didn't matter. What mattered was that Dad said yes!

I was excited to be an official Brownie Scout. Mom was a Brownie troop leader. As I moved up the ranks, so did she. Mom was the best Brownie troop ever! She had a way with the girls; they all loved her so much. I was proud to be her daughter. We enjoyed earning our badges, doing community services, and going on adventures with mom. I was amazed

That is a bit... It just doesn't set right

?

how Mom managed to be so active with her stoma. She never allowed it to be an excuse or to impair her from fulfilling her responsibilities. I look back now and realize that she held her own even during the days when her medical condition was challenging her.

I do not like may have taken her

When we went camping with the Scouts, I had to assist mom when she went to the outdoor toilets. It was cold, and there was no clean running water. Mom had to bring water with her to rinse out her colostomy bag. I stood outside the door to make sure no one would bust in on her. When the other girls would ask me why I always had to go with her when she went to the toilet, I would protectively say, "She's my mother!" They asked no further questions.

Mom always kept a special bag packed with a spare outfit for any unexpected moments. She was never caught off her guard or unprepared. She lived ready for life to throw her a curveball at any time but she was already with a goal of hitting a home run. Even if I only make it to first base." To this day, I carry that spare outfit with me in my bag.

Nightmare in Montana

Our travel across the US was a challenge for dad. We didn't know how bad it was until we got older. It was during the end of the civil rights era. There was civil unrest in some areas of the country along the way. We were stationed in tiny, remote towns that were predominantly populated with White people. These were often mean, evil-minded White people who did not like the fact that a Black family was moving into their neighborhoods. Dad would often tell us how to behave around them.

"You do not have to address adults with 'Yes ma'am' and 'Yes sir,' he told us. "Call them 'Mr. and Mrs." and use their proper name."

I was so happy about that because when I was told to say, "Yes ma'am," I proudly would say, "My dad told me I didn't have to. All I have to say is 'Mr. and Mrs.' and your last name." It would get me out of trouble every time.

Going to school in Montana was hard for me. The building was small, and the teachers were insensitive to cultural differences. I was teased and ridiculed because of the color of my skin and never acknowledged for the character of my being. I worked hard, hoping to be recognized for my schoolwork or citizenship. Still, I never got the acknowledgment I wanted while living there.

My mother made me a pretty blue gingham dress. I wore it to school one day. I sat across from this little boy who constantly poked me with his pencil. He would call me names under his breath. The teacher never seemed to notice him bothering me. Every time I would tell the teacher, he never got in trouble for it. One day, while I had my head down on my desk, per the teacher's request, he started poking me again. My dress had a hole in the seam of my underarm. Suddenly, I felt a sharp stab in my armpit. He had poked his pencil directly into the hole of my sleeve.

"Stop it!" I screamed out.

I suffered through this

Wow!

:)

lol

"Stop what?" He said.

The teacher asked me to explain the reason I yelled out in class. I was too embarrassed to tell her I had a hole in the underarm of my dress. So, I just told her he was bothering me without any details. That wasn't enough to get me out of trouble for disrupting the classroom. The teacher sent me to the principal's office. During those times, it was permissible to give a student a few smacks on the hand with a ruler if they misbehaved in class.

When they called to let dad know I was in trouble, he headed straight to the school. I was so proud when he walked in wearing his Air Force uniform. He looked so regal, standing six feet four inches tall looking down at the principal sitting at his desk. I explained to dad what happened.

"The next time that little boy touches my daughter, she has my permission to knock some sense into him. Then the school will have to deal with me!" He told the principal, right in front of me.

When we got in the car to drive home, dad added, "If that boy pokes you with his pencil again, you have permission to poke his eyeballs out with your pencil." I laughed at dad's comments. I knew he was talking out of frustration.

The next day I couldn't wait to get back to school so that I could have a reason to poke that boy with my pencil in return for all the times he had been poking me. I took full advantage of Dad's permission to handle my business whenever I felt bullied or picked on because of the color of my skin. Dad said as long as I didn't hit first or throw the first punch, it was self-defense. It was essential to protect myself at all costs. I never lost a fight. *Oh wow!*

Fighting the Good Fight

In Montana, Leroy and I took a school bus 40 miles to the small, white-painted school we attended. I was in the 3rd grade, and he was in the 5th grade. At school, we were treated like we weren't worthy of a fair and equal educational experience. That bus ride was horrific! Every day we would sit in the same seat, clutching each other's hands as the bus took us far away from our peaceful domain at home. Leroy would be biting his lip in anger. I was ducking my head back and forth to avoid the paper wads, pencils, and other objects that were being thrown at us.

The kids' voices would grow louder and louder as we made our way down the bumpy road across the countryside of the Montana planes. They would say, "Hey niggers! Go back to Africa!" Or "Look at the ugly monkeys!" Those kids yelled obscenities at us for almost an hour each day. I often looked to see if the bus driver would come to our rescue, pull the bus over and demand that the kids stop it. He never did. Other times, I closed my eyes and prayed to God to make them shut up. They didn't. Finally, the bus came to an abrupt stop, and the squeaky doors opened at the school. As the kids walked off in single file, I would breathe a sigh of relief that we made it. School should have been a safe place. It wasn't. Struggling through the school day became harder. As the day drew to a close, Leroy and I dreaded getting back on the bus for that long ride back home. We decided to do something to stop the bullying.

After school, we entered the bus holding hands as usual and sat as close as we could to one another. Leroy pointed out two kids that always started the name-calling--a boy and girl.

"They get off at our same stop," he said. "Today, when they get off, you get the girl. I'll get the boy."

Once the bus ride was underway, the racial slurs became unbearable. It gave me inner courage to end this madness forever. Leroy and I got off the bus and waited for the two kids as the bus pulled away. I looked for the signal from Leroy. When he gave it, we beat those kids up until we were satisfied. Then we watched them run home, crying and yelling they were going to tell their parents. We didn't care. Leroy and I promised each other we would keep this a secret between the both of us.

Later that evening, after dinner, we heard a knock on the door. Dad opened it to find his boss standing in his military uniform. His son and daughter were with him, badly bruised from our fight. Dad called Leroy and me into the living room. He chastised us in front of his boss, made us ask forgiveness, and promised it wouldn't happen again. When they left, dad praised us for taking care of business.

"Next time, if there were to be one, make sure the kids aren't my bosses' children!" he said.

Leroy and I were proud of ourselves for taking care of business. Things calmed down quickly as the word got around school not to mess with the McGees. The bus ride became bearable. I

This whole part really made me shed tears

owe all of that to my brother. He taught me how to stand up for myself as a girl and not be afraid of anyone, especially those with mean intentions. I had become sensitive to the way the world treated people who looked like me.

Murder of Dr. King

After leaving Montana, we moved back to Oklahoma. This time we lived in Midwest City, Oklahoma, for a short time. Dad had received orders to be stationed in Cold Bay, Alaska. We stayed in Oklahoma until he completed his assignment. One day, as I played in my room, I heard my mother cry out, "OH GOD NO!"

I rushed into the living room and noticed she was watching TV. She continued to cry. It was the most hurtful cry I had ever heard from her. I glanced at the TV screen and saw a sea of Black people running around, buildings burning, and many police officers. I couldn't figure it out. I had to ask.

"Mom, what happened?"

She gathered herself for a moment and said, "Martin Luther King Jr. was shot and killed!"

I didn't yet know the magnitude of Dr. King's influence on the civil rights movement. I just knew if his death had caused my mother to react this way, then he had to be someone special. We both sat down in front of the TV for hours, watching the news coverage. The riots and protests were chilling to me. I cried for hours along with my mother. She held me as if she was protecting me from the world right outside our doors. I still feel that hug when I need protection. I didn't realize how profound the impact of his death was for her until I grew older and learned more about Dr. King himself. The more I learned about him, the more I became confused about why I wasn't taught about his incredible fight for human rights and racial justice in school. As I grew older, I processed my father's core value of doing something to make this society better than what it was when you arrived. He was trying to model Dr. King's mindset. The day I learned of MLK Jr.'s passing changed my life. I became so much more aware of why my parents provided a home filled with deep love and loyalty to each other. They set the example of Christian living and the expectation of showing acts of kindness. Outside of our home during those times, the nation seemed to be exercising the opposite of those values.

While Dad was in Alaska, Mom held down the fort. It was fun being raised by mom in dad's absence. She was not as strict as dad was. Her love for life made every day go by faster while he was away from us. We did a lot of fun things with her. She kept us busy as much as she could, keeping our minds occupied with positive and creative things. We were always at church and engaged in youth activities that kept us rooted in our Christian values. Mom always made the home feel warm and fuzzy. She cooked comfort meals and always topped them off with one of her homemade desserts. She maintained a routine schedule from sunrise to bedtime. Each night, she made her rounds to assure we said our prayers and to wish us sweet dreams. We all missed dad. Even though he wasn't physically with us, we knew that if mom gave him a negative report, we would be in a world of trouble when he got home. We tried to behave the way he expected us to act when he was at home with us. Mom depended on dad for our safety and security. She had to be the captain of the ship while he was away.

Twister in Oklahoma

One day, the radio informed us that a destructive tornado was headed toward Midwest City. I can still see the fear on my mom's face when I reimagine the moment. She told my siblings and me to go to a corner of the house and huddle up. She then wrapped her arms as much as she could around all of us. We had the radio on and were listening to the updates. They warned that the tornado was approaching rapidly.

"I think I can beat the tornado before it gets here," mom said.

Mom planned to drive about ten miles west to Oklahoma City, bringing us to safety with her church friends. We grabbed our things and ran for the car outside. Rain was hitting like rocks, while thunder and lightning shook the house like a bumper car. When we got in the car, the rain was coming down so hard and fast that mom couldn't see out the front window as she started the car. The windshield wipers were barely able to move back and forth. I heard mom crying and praying to God to let her get out of the city before the tornado arrived.

We only made a it block from the house before the wind started blowing strong enough to force our car to slide across the road. We could barely move forward against the wind gusts blowing fiercely in the direction we were headed. On the car radio, we heard the weatherman announce that the tornado had picked up speed and was due to hit our town at any moment. Mom decided to turn the car around in the middle of the street and head back home. She kept saying that she couldn't see anything.

"God, please help me get my children back home safely," she pleaded with God. I remember seeing the wipers bending back and forth across the windshield, causing little effect on mom's visibility. I looked directly at her face and saw a look of determination as she clutched the steering wheel at ten and two. Her shoulders were hunched forward in a tensed position as she maneuvered our car down the block toward the house. As we turned the corner, I could see our brick red house in the near distance. It felt like forever before we got to the driveway. She ushered us out of the car and into the house. She told us to run to the corner of the house and retake cover. She soon joined us with her portable radio. Suddenly, just as she completed another prayer, the wind and rain stopped, and a quietness settled in the air. The radio announced that the tornado had skipped over Midwest City and was headed to the other side of town.

Mom began shouting hallelujah praise, thanking God for saving her family. Once again, I witnessed a miracle because of my mom's prayers! Events like this as a young girl strengthened my faith and relationship with God. I learned that prayer could change circumstances beyond my control. I was young, but I was a believer in the real power of prayer. Later, Mom told me that if she had exercised more faith by staying in the house instead of trying to outrun the tornado. She wouldn't have gone through so much stress and caused us to worry about our safety.

"My prayers and faith would have been sufficient," she said. "God had everything in control. He would have fully protected our family. I was trying to do God's job as if He wasn't capable."

One of my favorite scriptures is Psalm 46:10: "Be still and know that I am God." I can only imagine how difficult it must have been for mom to do at the time. I have to admit this is one of the hardest things for me to do. I really wanted my dad to come home. I felt safer when he was with us, and I know it put a lot of stress on mom when he was away. She was managing four children, plus her medical condition. She never complained, but I could see how much she needed Dad with us.

Dad wrote us letters while in Alaska. He told us how cold it was there and how much he missed being with his family. His notes included firm instructions to do what we needed to do to help mom out while he was away. The best part about receiving the letters was the $1 bill he sent with it. It felt like it was the golden ticket! He was the best dad in the whole world. With the gift of that dollar, I knew he also had to be the richest dad in the universe!

Less than a year after the tornado scare, Dad came home. We united as a family again. He said it was too cold in Alaska and he hated being so far away from us. Now it was time for us to move on to Morro Bay, California.

LETTERS FROM DAD DURING
HIS TIME IN ALASKA

A gift for being a sweet girl
$1.00

TSGT W. J. McGee
Cold Bay Alaska
11 Oct 1968

Mrs Cynthia McGee

To the sweet one in the McGee
family, thanks for the wonderful letter you
wrote me I really did enjoy it and
I was suprise to hear from you but I
should not have been because I knew
you would write because I know you
love me as I love you.

The weather isn't really cold here yet
but it will be soon and when it get
real cold I'll put on so many clothes that
I'll look like the fat man.

Did you have a good time at the
fair? I'm sorry I didn't have a chance
to take you before I had to leave but you
know I had no choice because the day we
were going to the fair it started to rain
and we could not go while it was raining.

That is good news about you being
in the school choir and your mother told
me that you are doing good in school well
keep up the good work and remember
I love very much
Your Daddy
W. J. McGee

LETTERS FROM DAD DURING
HIS TIME IN ALASKA

W Jms Dee
Cold bay alaska

Miss Cynthia

Sometime words fail to say things as they should be said and when I try to say how much I love you, I find I don't have the words to say it as it should be said. So here is a little gift to help me say it. And maby this gift will also say I will be glad to come home, and that I miss you very much.

please be a good ~~gift~~ young lady, and give your mother all the help she ned around the house, because she ned it.

Rmember I still love you and I know you love me. please write me soon.

your. daddy mc.Gee

Black Culture

On our way to California, we stopped in Texas to visit my mom's family. My mom's family was a classic example of real Black cultural living. When we came to visit, all of her siblings were there. They called mom Eddie Mae and gave her ultimate respect. My grandfather, Fate Dotson, was loud talking and fair-skinned like my mom. He didn't hold back his bold opinion on any topic at hand. He used profanity at will and never pulled any punches when it came to how he felt about anything, especially his family's love and protection. He was short in stature, bow-legged, and physically fit. He was missing his entire middle finger and half of his pointer finger on his right hand. When he smoked, he held his cigarette between his thumb and his ring fingers. He talked loudly as if he was trying to make sure they heard his voice across town. He scared me when I first met him. I was standing back observing his behavior. After he caught me doing so, he yelled, "Get over here and hug him, dammit!" When I made my way over to him, he gave me the most endearing hug I had ever felt. I was immediately in awe of my grandfather. He made me laugh at how he talked. He always seemed angry to me. After I got to know him, I saw that he was kind, yet serious about life.

My grandmother Jonnie Lee Dotson was a dark-skinned slender woman who was very intriguing to observe. She spoke with a light, raspy-sounding voice but had a deep gentleness about herself. Her hair was pressed and combed straight back into a short ponytail. She also smoked cigarettes. I had never seen a woman smoke until I met her. She came over to me and gave me a warm hug.

"You're Eddie Mae's oldest daughter, huh?" she said.

"Yes," I said proudly.

"Uh-huh," she replied. She looked me up and down and then said, "You are a big girl. You help your mom out around the house?"

I proudly said, "Yes", again.

She replied, "That's good." Then she patted me on the head and walked into the kitchen. I wanted to follow her, but dad had not permitted us to explore the environment. In other words, we couldn't move.

Grandmother didn't have much to say. Granddaddy did most of the talking or fussing. I guess she felt his voice was enough most of the time. When I heard her speak, she was giving instructions or making a short comment toward something significant. Granddaddy started and carried most conversations. Grandmother finished them. The commotion was wild when the house was filled with every one of my mom's siblings plus our family of six. People were laughing, smoking, cussing, fussing, and playing the dozens with one another. I thought they were saying the rudest things to each other, but the comments were so funny they made me laugh inside my head a few times. I had never heard family talk about each other like that before. In our family, that wasn't allowed. It was a culture shock for me. I dared myself not to laugh out loud. Getting into adult conversations would get me into big trouble. Mom and dad were catching up on life with everyone. We were doing what children were supposed to do back in the day--"Be seen and not heard." I was busy checking out every cultural difference in my mom's family and comparing it to ours. My head was swiveling from left to right, up and down. People were in conversations from the living room to the front porch. They were arguing in one moment and laughing together in the next. My ears were taking in all the new sounds--the chickens in the backyard, the pots and pans, laughing and fussing in the kitchen, dogs barking, and loud music playing in cars that drove by. I could hear the air conditioner rattling in the window, spitting a mist of cool water back into the house. I wanted to sit in front of that air conditioner, it was a scorching hot and muggy day in Texas. However, my Aunt Theresa, who was pregnant at the time, was lying on a twin bed under the air conditioner. She looked too comfortable to share her space. After a while, my uncles Bennie and Larry asked my father's permission to take my sisters to the store to show off their cute nieces. Dad gave them strict instructions on a timeframe and the places they were not to take them. My brother Leroy left with my Uncle Fred, who gave dad a thumb's up signal that meant, "I got it." I was left standing in the middle of the room. I felt like the little black sheep or the runt of the family. I held back my tears. My mom asked me if I was ok. She knew.

I was about to break down about being left behind when my Aunt Marie also noticed and told me to come with her. She led me into a bedroom across from the living room. Mom followed her.

Marie and my mom were the closest of their siblings in age and in their relationship. They had a special bond. That day, I got to listen to mom and Marie laugh together as they talked about many childhood memories. Aunt Marie has a contagious laugh. She loves to laugh just like I do. From the first time we met, we laughed together. We connected through laughter. They both gave me unspoken permission to listen and laugh with them even when some things were spoken in code. Aunt Marie made me feel special that day. She still holds a special place in my heart.

I also connected with my Aunt Theresa, who had dimples just like my mom. That hot day turned into a steamy, muggy night. I was complaining about how hot I was when it was time to go to bed. She heard me and told my mom to let me come lie down next to her under the air conditioner. She was at least five months pregnant and showing. I was afraid I was going to smash the baby in her stomach. When I told her that, she laughed and held me close to her belly all night.

There was a quiet young lady following my mom around the house, mumbling unhappy words under her breath. She was responding to being teased by her siblings. It was my Aunt Linda Jean, who is intellectually disabled. Aunt Linda Jean loved my mom, her big sister. I observed her role in the family and was impressed by how she managed her life. She knew she lived in a family that loved her in spite of her disability.

The next day, my granddaddy invited me into the kitchen to help him cook some beans and chicken. My mom must have shared with him how much I loved helping in the kitchen. I was given the task of picking out the bad beans and rinsing water over the good ones. When it was time to cook the beans, Granddaddy grabbed a large pot with a funny-looking lid. I now know it to be a pressure cooker. He poured the beans into the pot and added water. The pressure cooker rumbled and steamed for hours. Finally, Granddaddy released the pressure and like a locomotive engine, steam came shooting out. He yelled at me to get out of the way before I got burned. It was a sight to see. But those were the best-tasting beans I've ever had. Grandaddy was the cook of the family. He made the entire meal, which included southern fried chicken. It was the best meal. In fact, it was the last time I got a chance to eat his cooking with my grandparents. They both passed away, one month apart, after we arrived at our new home in Morro Bay, California.

We finally left Texas and continued on our trip to California. Mom and Marie cried when we departed. As a child we never lived near any extended family members on either side. As McGees, we had to learn how to depend on each other and to live in harmony with each other. When life seemed difficult, there wasn't a cousin to talk to or an Aunt's house to go over, or even a grandmother or grandfather to call. With us moving around so much, friends were far and in between. As a family, we figured life out together. Dad did a great job at setting up the expectation and execution of family synergy. Mom layered it with empathy. One could not exist without the other-- synergy and empathy. Dad sealed our family bond with his diligent provision and mom with her unconditional love. I have never let go of that expectation dad had for our family. I couldn't define it as a child but as I grew up, I realized how much I held myself accountable for maintaining our vital family bond throughout the years.

Dad was stationed in Cambridge Air Force Base in Cambria, which is located in the mountains in northern California. He didn't want us to live on the base there, so we lived south of Cambria in Morro Bay. It was beautiful. We lived about three blocks from the beach. Yet again, we were in an all-White neighborhood. Dad found a church in San Luis Obispo. We would take a 40-mile drive there from Morro Bay every Sunday. We had to get up so early to arrive in time for Sunday School. By the time we got there, I was so tired, I'd be half asleep through Sunday School and the main service. I hardly remember anything about our church experience except there were Black people that we never got a chance to know. As soon as church was over, we left to take the long drive back home. We slept, coming and going, leaving every Sunday memory on the freeway along the way. Soon I think dad and mom got tired of taking the trip. Our membership at that church was short lived.

Mom was devastated when she learned of her father passing. One month later, her mother also passed. She cried for months. I thought she would never stop mourning her parents passing. Granddaddy was a construction worker. He fell on a live wire and was electrocuted. Then almost to the date a month later in November her mother passed. Grandmother died from a brain aneurysm, in her home.

My siblings and I did not get a chance to go to their memorial services. Mom told me how difficult the funeral was for all of her siblings. She told me that she never wants her children to experience that much pain from losing her or my dad. I didn't understand why mom would say that. As far as I was concerned, the pain would be unbearable if she or dad ever died. At that point, I made up in my mind that she and dad were going to live forever. I couldn't deal with the fact that everyone alive will inevitably pass away. Time eventually allowed healing to take place. After many months, mom seemed to be back to her old self. She was smiling and laughing again.

New Horizons in Morro Bay

During our travel across the country on our way to Morro Bay, I remember Dad stopping to get us something to eat at a drive-in. Back then, after you ordered your food, the servers would bring it out on a tray and hang it on your car window. Well, this time, after the lady brought the food out, she told dad that he had to take his family around to the back of the drive-in to eat. Colored folks weren't allowed to eat in the front. Suddenly, Dad threw the food on the ground and sped off down the street, burning rubber. As the tires were spinning, the smell of burnt rubber took over the fresh burger and crispy hot French fry aroma. As we drove away, my head snapped back to see the food splattered all over the ground. Then my head swiveled around to watch dad managing the car like he was in the last lap of the Indy 500 race. Finally, my eyes shifted to mom yelling

Racism

at dad, begging him to slow down before the police came. He was so mad; I was so hungry.

We all sat quietly, awaiting dad's decision of where the next stop for food would be. It felt like we were on the road forever as dad drove to the next town. When we arrived, dad assured us that he would be getting us something to eat. This time he went into the place, ordered the food, and brought it out to the car in brown paper bags. I could see the grease markings indicating that there had to be some delicious French fries in there. Yum! He handed the food to mom, started the car, and drove off without saying a word.

As mom handed the food to her starving kids, dad explained that he would never accept his family being treated as if we were slaves. Dad recounted that experience often by saying, "Always have enough money to buy what you can afford. Never let someone treat you less than you deserve to be treated." He felt that if we had eaten at the drive-in, it would have taught us to sacrifice our dignity and accept lesser treatment because we were Black.

I felt so proud of my dad that day. I packed that lesson in my conscience and the experience in my heart. I carry it with me on my journey to remind me how hard my dad worked to give us the tools we need to be respected as Black members of this society. My dad was an incredibly proud and dignified Black man. He responded to that challenge the same way he navigated his journey walking off the cotton field as a teenager. However, that time he had his family with him and wanted to teach us to never accept less than what we deserve but work harder to get what we desire.

Child's Play

A couple of my fondest memories in Morro Boy included times we went down to the beach and built a clubhouse with my brother and sister. We discovered an old tree that had fallen over near dry land off the street, near a pathway leading down to the beach area. We swept the sand away as much as we could, creating a flat surface to put blankets on the ground where we sat and ate. The tree hung over our heads like a mushroom of protection and a secret hiding place from the outside world. We would go there every day possible after school, and on weekends. We could hear the sounds of the ocean tide and the seagulls. The chill of the northern winds made our bodies and teeth shiver in unison. One day, a winter storm came and destroyed our clubhouse. Sand had rushed back in, covering up our neatly cleaned floor. Our blankets were soaked, and branches of the tree had broken off exposing our once hidden treasure. We never got a chance to rebuild it before we left Morro Bay.

Esther and I begged dad to build us a playhouse on the side of the garage in the back of the house instead. Finally, one day, we saw dad with cardboard and wood. He was building us a playhouse! Soon after it was finished, we got a grand idea. Instead of playing in it we decided to create an Indian Village. We knew nothing significant about Native Americans, beyond what we saw watching Cowboy and Indian movies with my mother. In our minds, the playhouse resembled a flat-topped tee-pee. Outside, we set up places where they smashed the corn they harvested and rocks where they washed their clothes, and a campfire to cook their food. It was strictly something we made up. Inside, we created a place to sleep. We wrapped our dolls up like papooses. We also created a daily routine, where we imagined that the men were out hunting for food. We, the women were home and picking berries. We were pretending to prepare the home with everything needed to prepare a decent meal for the men who were out hunting it down. Then we made flyers and charged neighbors a minimal amount to come see the Indian Village, created and designed by the McGee sisters. We had examples of clothing, and food to taste. People actually came to see our village! It was the most people we had seen out of their homes at one time in the neighborhood. Esther and I traded off collecting money and giving tours at our back gate. It was so much fun. We created this world for Native Americans just using our childish imaginations. People were donating money, dropping it into our shoebox to show their support. It was my first community event that ignited the passion in me to bring people together to understand those who are different.

Best Friend

We had been in Morro Bay for over a year and a half when mom and dad began pushing me to find my gift or land on a pathway to fulfilling my dreams. I was interested in being involved in school clubs and being active in sports. So, when my brother entered track and field, I followed. I was a sprinter and ran the 40-yard dash and relay races. I also did the short jump. Joining the track team in Morro Bay provided an opportunity to feel like I was accepted and respected by my peers. I was finally on the same team as them. I ran well and really enjoyed it. My brother told me I had a fast start, but the "hawk" would get me near the end of the race. Once I got to the finish line, I constantly gasped for air and had a hard time relaxing into a regular breathing pattern. Mom, who attended every track meet, would come to the field and make me breathe into a brown paper bag until my breathing settled down. It was so embarrassing! Dad never attended the track meets. He was always working. Leroy was incredible at track and field. He won ribbons for his sprints, relays, the long jump, and triple jump events. He was popular at our school, and he made friends with ease. It was harder for me to make friends. Dad made friends with a family named the Parkers. They were the first Black family we would visit in Morro Bay. They had three children, all of whom were younger than us--Hallick, Curtis Jr., and Christina. We had fun visiting with them.

One day, things suddenly changed to my benefit. I met a friend named Becky, who lived on the opposite side of the neighborhood in a custom-built home. Becky and I were junior Girl Scouts, and we both had dreams of becoming cadets together. Mom was still a troop leader. Becky's mother was also a troop leader, and they got along well.

Becky was a thin girl. I would have called her boney. She had shoulder-length, wavy blond hair and long blond eyelashes. I had never seen eyelashes as blond as hers. Her junior Girl Scouts uniform never quite fit her well. It hung off her body like it was still on a hanger in her closet. With all the badges sewn on, her sash seemed to weigh her frail body down when she adorned it across her shoulder.

Becky always wanted to understand how I felt when our peers made fun of the color of my skin and treated me unkindly in school. Going to school in Morro Bay was lonely and scary because it was so big. Once again, I was the only Black girl there. Becky and I would talk about our differences. It seemed to bring us together rather than pull us apart. Becky was compassionate. I appreciated that. I trusted her and never questioned her friendship. We would work together on completing our badges at her house. She never came to my house. In retrospect, I believe her parents didn't let her because of how she might have gotten treated by her other friends. Her parents probably didn't want to be questioned by their prejudiced peers in the neighborhood. I was just happy I finally knew what it felt like to have a friend. Becky taught me the magic of keeping a diary and often shared hers with me. However, I had to make a pinky promise of secrecy, so I won't share what she wrote in it.

Our friendship was short-lived. Dad soon got orders to move to Mt. Laguna Air Force Base in Southern California. I was sad when we left. I even cried. We made a Girl Scouts promise to write to each other. We did for a while, then we lost contact. She was the first White friend I had. To this day, I measure friendship compared to the precious moments we shared during the short time we knew each other.

El Cajon is No Hollywood

Dad left for Southern California a few months before we did. He said he would secure a house for us and get acquainted with the city where we would live. When dad came back for us, I was excited to explore our new destination. I was also becoming weary from uprooting my life every two years. I didn't know that we were headed to another challenging experience living in the city of El Cajon, California.

My brother looked forward to pursuing his passion for sports. He was getting to a handsome age, and he was feeling himself. Girls were starting to give him "jock" attention. I was going into the 7th grade and still hadn't reached a level of social maturity compared to my middle school peers. I was still very focused on being the caretaker of my family. I held on to this sense of obligation to ensure that Mom and Dad's synergy created within the McGee family was present. The love we shared for one another secured our bond. After saying the Lord's prayer every night, I would end with saying every member of my family by name.

"God bless Mom, Dad, Leroy, Cynthia, Esther, and Baby Sister forever and ever. Amen."

I never could imagine anything destroying our bond. I always felt that my family was so tightly bonded together in love and respect. But now, I deeply longed to experience respect and love from outside of my family. I had a difficult time finding it in these predominantly White neighborhoods, where others disrespected my Blackness. Life was about to get real!

Traveling from Northern California to Southern California was short compared to the other trips we made back and forth across the country. All of my siblings and I were piled in the back of our new blue station wagon when dad woke us up. He announced that we were in San Diego and had about 15 miles to go before we reached our new home in El Cajon. As one head popped up at a time, we took a squinty-eyed look outside the car windows. We were in awe of the sight. We came in on the Interstate-8 freeway and were going through an area called Mission Valley. It was the holiday season, and there were lights on the hillsides and in the valley. We passed a large shopping center that was bright with stores filled with holiday decorations. The vast parking lots were packed with cars and people were bustling around. We drove through another town or two before we rounded the bend into the city of El Cajon. It was amazing! Bright twinkling lights covered the valley floor and ran up to the surrounding hills and into the mountainsides where homes were nestled deep in prime real estate. My siblings and I screamed and yelled like we had been transported to the middle of Hollywood. Dad chuckled at us as he exited Main Street. As we moved through the center of town, the night grew darker, hindering us from a clear vision of our drive to "Hollywood." He finally drove into the parking lot of an apartment complex. Dad told us to quiet down as we gathered our things and made our way to the lower-level apartment door. The apartment was fully furnished, and our rooms were set up to welcome our arrival. We fell asleep in anticipation of seeing our Hollywood in the morning. Dad left for work very early the following day because he had almost an hour drive east to his job at Mount Laguna Air Force Base. After I ate breakfast, I got dressed in neatly pressed clothes and combed my hair in a style that resembled transitioning from grade school to middle school. Then, I opened our door. To my disappointing surprise, there was a small shabby looking playground right outside our front door. It didn't look inviting to play in at all. It didn't matter to Baby Sister, who wanted to go out to swing. I volunteered for playground duty. Esther joined us, and Leroy stayed inside the apartment. He was too cool to explore the childish surroundings.

We played outside until a few White children came and asked why we were there and who let us play in their playground. They told us that they were going to tell their parents and get us kicked out of there. I told them we lived there and that my little sister could play here if she wanted. Esther stood by my side in support until they left. We soon went inside and told mom what happened. When Dad came home, I asked him what happened to Hollywood and all the beautiful lights?" The apartment complex was ugly, and the area looked dry and dirty. I was thankful the apartment had a pool, but I was afraid to even get in it based on how the children had treated us in that shabby playground. I was expecting to live in a house or on base in housing that looked clean and orderly. I didn't feel comfortable with this type of living. He explained that we would only be there until an available house came up through the base housing commission. I was glad to hear that it settled my anxiety for a while.

The following day we found a note taped to the front door requesting that we leave the apartment complex. It said other tenants felt unsafe and didn't want their kids playing with us in the playground. Dad marched that note to the manager's office and told him that he would report it to his commander. He said he and his family were not going anywhere until the military moved us! Dad told us to go outside and play whenever we wanted and let him know if anyone gave us a problem. He was so angry.

Dad further explained that he wasn't serving in the military for his family to be treated poorly by the very people he was protecting through his service. He was proud of serving his country and was deeply patriotic. We were forced to follow his lead in that mindset. We were never to disrespect his oath and call to duty through our actions or words, so I knew he wouldn't allow anyone else to. I couldn't wait for Christmas break to end and for school to start so that I could focus on something more exciting than this negative atmosphere.

TomGirl

I loved running. To bond with us as kids, dad would challenge my siblings and me to race him on our street block. I loved accepting the challenge, even though my short-legged strides were no match to my dad's was 6'4" long-legged strides. It gave him an advantage for a victorious win every time! To provide me with false hopes of winning, he would allow me a long head start. Then, like Roadrunner, flash past me, laughing sarcastically. It was so much fun racing dad in hopes of capturing a win that never happened. He never allowed me to come close to an inch of his heels during a race. Dad was not athletic and didn't pretend to be. He was proud that he never played organized sports because he claimed that his intelligence gave him the advantage in life he needed. He used racing to express his powerful ability to control his position as patriarch of our family. He always captured the lead. I used racing to chase after the attention and love I needed and wanted from him.

Dad didn't express a daddy-daughter type of love with me. I can't remember him ever sitting me on his lap and telling me what a beautiful little girl I was unless mom put the words into his mouth. He rarely complimented how I looked in a new dress, no matter how much I danced around in front of him, trying to capture his attention. I longed for special affirmation that surpassed the praise I constantly received from him for being a good helper for mom.

Dad was stern and serious about how he wanted me to act like a girl growing up. He required me to sit, walk, talk and act like a lady. Dad was hard on me because I had tomboy tendencies. I loved hanging on to my mother's skirt tail, learning how to be domestic. I also loved being outdoors, climbing trees, big rocks, running around creating adventures. I explored my ability to challenge my physical strength against any fear or opposition that came my way. Boys never treated me like a tender-hearted little girl. I played marbles and other games with them and with my brother. As I grew older, in school I became the keeper of everyone's secret crushes and was soon promoted to become the mail carrier of love notes and messages to the girls and boys that liked each other. I never got love letters, though. I wasn't lucky or maybe pretty enough to capture the heart of the boys. Besides, I was Black. They were White. In those days, it was taboo. So, even if I was the object of a childhood crush, I was never aware of it.

I have a bold laugh. It is authentic. It starts in the depth of my ticklish core. It grows into a boisterous chuckle exiting through my vocal cords with a distinctive cadence that swells in maximizing volume until I reach personal satisfaction. Dad was annoyed by my laugh. It drew unwanted attention, and he would tell me it wasn't lady-like. He would always try to quiet me by calling out my name in a disapproving way—"CYN-THIA!" He would often sit me down in front of him and make me practice laughing in a dainty manner with my hand over my mouth, forcing me to lower my volume to a whisper. It was frustrating at first. Then it became funny to me every time he tried teaching me how to laugh. I couldn't help but laugh harder and louder every time he tried. Sometimes he would break down and laugh with me. Eventually, he gave up, and I was free to laugh without restraint. My laugh became my claim to fame. Dad's effort to control my laughter was ironic to me. He loved humor himself. In fact, he had such a deep love for comedy that he would gather the whole family around his long maple wood console record player and play albums of Bill

Cosby's standup monologues for hours. It was the family time dad so proudly set aside for us.

Bonding and synergy continued to grow to define the unique dynamics of our family, which meant so much to him. Laughing together allowed a way to release and decompress from the stresses of living during the civil rights era and beyond. When times were difficult in our society, at work, in our schools, at church, and even within the family, laughter healed and comforted us. Dad never tried to stifle the range of laughing cadence that rang out as we all sat among each other, munching on a plate of snacks mom prepared during our family time. We used our imagination and visionary senses to follow Bill Cosby's comedic scenarios. After years of doing this, I knew most of the punch lines and could tell the stories, impersonating Cosby's voice. To this day, I love telling stories and creating character voices to enhance the humor in the story. In essence, it's my dad's fault that laughter is such an essential part of my life because he introduced it to me, and I packed it into my bag. He just couldn't influence or change how I exercised laughing.

Tragedy Strikes

Tragedy hit the McGee Household. One day, mom told me dad was in a car accident while he was driving home from work. The drive to Mount Laguna was a winding two-lane road that wound across both sides of the mountain. Dad carpooled with a fellow Airman. That day Dad was driving. While driving down the mountainside, the car's steering wheel locked up. Dad crashed into the rocky side of the mountain. The car hit it on the passenger side. The Airman was severely hurt. Dad gave him mouth-to-mouth resuscitation for 45 minutes before the medics showed up. The Airman died at the scene of the accident. Dad had minor injuries. He was off work for a while, healing from both his physical pain and emotional trauma. I remember trying to talk to him about it, but he cut the conversation short. Mom kept me informed with the details. For the rest of his life, I never heard another word about the accident from him. I used to wonder if it was because he had incredible resolve or because he was incredibly weakened by the experience. I don't wonder anymore.

Coming of Age

As I grew up in the McGee household, I became keenly aware of the different personalities starting to emerge. My siblings were becoming individuals instead of a collected group of enlisted troops dad had complete control of. I was entering Junior High School, and my brother was on his way to High School. Esther was in 6th grade, and Baby Sister was just beginning 1st grade. Dad seemed to have ambitions of advancement in the Air Force. Mom was fully engaged in supporting all of our individual pathways. She quietly put all of her aspirations aside to assure our success.

We had arrived in El Cajon during the winter school break. I was used to cold weather and even snow during the winter months. It was sweltering hot there. The sun was shining every day, with no rain or snow clouds in the sky. The wind was hot and dry. They called them "Santa Ana winds." It was so different from any of the places we lived before. Soon it was time to enroll in school. I didn't need an oversized winter coat, rain, or snow boots. Just a light jacket, tennis shoes, and the new skirt mom made for me. I tucked my blouse neatly into the waist of my modest-length skirt, combed my pressed hair into two low hanging ponytails with bangs, and I was out the door headed to my new school. Upon arrival at school, I'd roll my skirt up to a less modest length, as mini-skirts were the style then.

Mom had to get all of us enrolled in school, and she had quite a hectic job doing so. When we got to my school, I noticed that there were still no Black students there. I was disappointed and soon became angry. Mom tried talking me out of my feelings but soon realized that a few words of loving support would do the trick. I remember the front office had a high counter. I could barely see the forehead of the Admissions Clerk. She tried her best to make me feel welcome and was doing a decent job until the Vice Principal appeared standing over me with his arms folded. He had a shiny bald head with a permanent like frown etched into his face. He stood at least 6'2" tall. He resembled Mr. Clean, without the wink and a smile. He introduced himself and immediately started to run off a long list of behavior rules and punishments if broken. This didn't scare me because living in the McGee home was like being in a military camp, and broken rules were met with corporal punishments. Dad didn't pull any punches when it came to misbehaving. Even though we were good kids 99% of the time, that 1% was met with heavy consequences that most of the time hardly matched the offense. Dad would tell us that if we broke the law and the police called him, he would let them keep us even if we were innocent. He said that meant that. We should never allow ourselves to be in any situation that would cause the police to be involved. So, I've never been arrested or been to jail. I avoided being anywhere the police could be involved. Well, at least I tried really hard to.

I hated that school and hated the Vice Principal with a passion. One day, I was eating a bag of corn chips in the outside lunch yard. I was having a fun time with a few students who were sitting at the table. Suddenly I pulled a burnt corn chip out of the bag and, in disgust, tossed it over my shoulder into the dirt next to me. I was not thinking about littering at all. The Vice Principal walked up to me and yelled, *"WHERE DO YOU THINK YOU ARE? I DON'T KNOW WHERE YOU CAME FROM, BUT THIS IS NOT A JUNKYARD. GET DOWN THERE AND PICK IT UP AND PROPERLY THROW IT IN THE TRASH WHERE IT BELONGS!"*

Everyone froze, and all eyes were on me. I got down on my knees and dug around in the dirt until I found the burnt corn chip. He followed me as I walked over to the trash can and threw it away. No one moved or said a word while all this was happening. After I finished, I sat down at the lunch table and worked hard to hold back my tears. When I get angry, I cry. I regretted my carelessness but hated how he handled it. When I told my mom, she went to the school and complained to the principal about how that made me feel. She said that because I was a Black student at the school, he should not have made a spectacle of me in such a degrading way. The Principal apologized to me on behalf of the Vice-Principal, but it was not enough to make me feel safe.

Mother joined the PTA and volunteered for various school events to show her presence and keep an eye on the Vice-Principal. I remember thinking that day I wanted to be a mother like her. I'd always make sure my children were protected by positioning myself in the direct path of anyone trying to hurt or harm them. I packed that mindset and waited many years to exercise it on my journey through life. Thanks, mom, for carrying a shield of love and protection over me.

Mother was a feisty Texas gal! She was not as composed as our dad. Her voice elevated to a high pitch when she became angry. She would use the funniest combination of Ebonics expressions! Sometimes dad would correct her pronunciation when she spoke. It frustrated mom because she felt like he always wanted her to rise above the cultural background and identity she was most comfortable and proud of. Dad was critical and corrected our use of the English language. He constantly corrected us and made us look up words to define our communication intent. I remember how critical he was one day when mom was asking me to find something for her. She told me it was "up under the sink." Before she could finish her sentence, Dad said, "Eddie, it can't be up and under. It either has to be up or under, not both."

It made me stop and think for a second. Just as it was making some sense to me, mom became frustrated and repeated her instructions, "As I said, Cynthia, it is up under the sink in a blue jar." I laughed at mom's response. But was smart enough not to laugh out loud enough for dad to hear me. I was proud of mom because she held her own and didn't allow dad to dictate her communication style with me. However, I never say "up under" to this day.

I eventually recognized how mom identified and stayed authentic to her Black cultural upbringing. She wanted us to remain authentic in our Blackness while being raised in a White society. On the other hand, Dad wanted us to learn how to survive as Black people in a White society. As we grew older, I noticed our home becoming the training center for learning how to survive by assimilation into White culture. It was so confusing to me because we lived in a White community and attended White schools. But we attended church in the Black community. In retrospect, I understand what dad's intention was. Still, I became angry trying to find my happy place in a culture where I was Black looking through White eyes.

I was entering my teen years. My body was going through puberty. My mind was developing by way of moving from the emotional use of my brain to critical thinking. I was starting to see life through my own lenses more than my parent's lenses. I was challenged with moving from a position of being the caretaker to taking care of myself. It was a strange time for me, and I didn't feel free enough to break out of that functional role in my family. Quite frankly, I didn't. I became more and more entrenched in making sure I was whatever my family needed or wanted me to be for them. Therefore, I paid less attention to developing into a confident teenager because of my insecurity and inability to trust that I could be comfortable living outside of the role I created for myself. I was conditioned to believe that if I did step out of that role, I would fail miserably and lose my identity in the family. To be totally transparent, if I had asked my family a long time ago if they wanted me to be this self-acclaimed caretaker for them, they probably would have told me no. I guess I was too afraid to hear or accept that answer. So, I never asked them even to this day. We were all growing, even my parents. Leroy and Esther had become strong, independent characters, so Mom and Baby Sister became my focus. They were my excuse to focus less on me and more on them. Baby Sister especially admired my attention to her personal needs and sometimes her spoiled demands. Mom simply needed my emotional support as she struggled with finding her independence in her marriage.

Working Mom

Mom started to gain her independence from her all-consuming role of caring for our family in El Cajon. She began looking for a part-time job to make her own money. Most of the women she met in the church and at the school functions had their own money to do as they wished. Mom always had to ask dad for money; she was growing tired of doing so. One day, she applied to work at a convenience store called Lavickio's, less than a block from our apartment. When she got the job as a cashier, she was elated. Mom loved her job. It was sometimes difficult for her to manage the register during busy periods in the store, but she always smiled and allowed her charismatic personality to soothe her impatient customers. One day, I came to the store to buy some candy. Mom seemed flustered by an annoyed customer who was waiting for mom to count out her change. Then I noticed irritation on another customer's face--a teenage boy. I watched him step up to the counter and complain about his wait in line. My anger boiled over when he began to disrespect my mom.

"Shut your mouth!" I yelled, stepping in front of him.

"Shut up nigger!" he exclaimed back.

I slowly turned, inch by inch, step by step. Then, like a Black girl with superpowers, I lunged across the floor to knock the daylight out of him. In the process, I knocked over a large wire cage of beach balls and other items on the counter in my pursuit of him. I wanted to snatch the breath out of his chest for daring to call me a nigger. Two other customers immediately grabbed me. They separated me from the boy and moved him to the other side of the store. My mom told me to pick up the beach balls, which were now all over the store. Frustrated, I quickly put them back in the wire bin and straightened up the counter. Then I waited for further instructions from mom. She told me to go home and that she would see me later. She worked for the rest of her shift. When she arrived home, all she did was shake her head in amusement. I tried explaining myself, but she cut me off.

"Thank you for trying to protect me," she said in a laughing manner. Then, with a serious tone, she added, "If I hadn't worked there, they might have called the police and charged me for any damage in the store. Luckily, they didn't. You could have gotten hurt or arrested fighting that boy."

"I don't care!" I responded. "Mom, I wanted to really hurt him." It was true. I wanted him to know that his White privilege ended the moment he took liberties to exercise it in the form of disrespect to you and to me." My family instilled a sense of pride and protection in me. I was glad to reach into my bag, grab it, and knock some sense into that boy.

Ready to Date

After I turned 17 years old, I asked my mom if she thought I was old enough to date.

"I think so," she said, "but you need to ask your dad."

I pondered and rehearsed how I would ask dad for permission to date. When I thought I was ready, I approached him while he was working on his car in the garage. I saw that he had his head deep under the hood of the vehicle. I was relieved that I didn't have to make eye contact with him. I perched myself on a stool across from him in the garage and crossed my legs in a confident, mature manner, clearing my voice.

"Dad, can I ask you a question?" I said. He did not look up.

"Yeah, go ahead," he said.

"Can I have permission to date?" He still didn't look up.

"Why do you want to date?" he replied.

My throat immediately dried up like I had a mouth full of salt rocks. I couldn't even swallow. My glands retreated to somewhere near my thumping heart. I wasn't prepared to provide a good reason.

"Well, everyone else my age is dating," was the best answer I could give.

With his head still under the hood of the car, he said, 'If everyone else was jumping off a cliff would you want to do the same?"

"No," I answered.

"Then you need to ask me that question when you are ready to give me a better reason for wanting to date. Then maybe I'll give you a better answer," he said. That was the end of that.

Months passed. I realized that dad wanted me to provide him with a logical reason for dating. I was soon to be a young adult. He had checked to see if my mindset was mature enough for the next phase of my life journey. I felt like I was ready, but I knew my dad wasn't. Dad and I never had that conversation again.

BLACK THROUGH
WHITE EYES

Always the Only

As time slowly passed, there was no improvement in how people treated us.

I asked my dad one day, "Why do we always have to be the only Black people in our neighborhood and school?"

"Because I work in a specialized field of service in the Air Force," he explained. "There aren't many Black men qualified to do this high level of work." Upady

"OK fine. Why don't you change your field of work so we can be around more people who look like us?" I replied. This question bothered dad, so he let me have it.

"That is not going to happen," he said sternly. "I studied long and hard to make it to this level of work. Also, I fully enjoy it.

You and the rest of the kids must learn to live under these circumstances. Figure out how to make the best of it without compromising who you are."

"Furthermore," he added, "because you are a little Black girl now and will soon be a Black woman, you need to remember that you will have to work three times harder than your White peers. You already have three strikes against you--one, being Black, two, being female, and three, being a McGee! For those reasons, you will have to do things differently. I expect you to be better and work harder than everyone else. That's how you will make a life for yourself. Don't ever ask me to change my field of work. My job allows me to feed you, clothe you, and provide a roof over your head. I am not going to change because you want life to be easier for you. Life wasn't easy on me but look what I accomplished!"

That was the end of that conversation. I have recounted it often. My dad taught me an essential lesson that I have carried throughout my lifetime. I recall his words every time I've seen challenging circumstances on the horizon or have been blindsided by a problem. I have persevered through many life obstacles by pulling that conversation out of my bag. Thank you, dad!

Instrumental Lessons

Dad insisted that Leroy, Esther, and I play an instrument. It wasn't optional.

104

I picked the cello, Esther chose the violin, and Leroy played the trumpet. In my beginning music class, I was surrounded by White students. It seemed that their parents had introduced them to instruments far before mine had. It seemed foreign to me. I had no idea why I picked the cello. It seemed like the instrument that only the strange and nerdy kids played. I wasn't good at all and struggled to impress my teacher. No one ever said that I could be a classical cello player or even encouraged me to become one. Instead, they said, "Honey, keep practicing."

My interest in the cello only lasted one year that culminated with a spring concert performance. I sat on the second-row. I barely made it through a couple of beginner songs. I faked reading the musical notes; I never got the hang of that. Instead, I memorized the songs by watching the other student's fingerboard placements. I followed the strokes they made on the strings, copying them on my cello with my bow. We had to bring our instruments home once a week to practice. I was so embarrassed walking home from school with my cello in its protective case strapped across my back as if I was carrying a dead body for burial. The White kids would make fun of me, jeering, "I never saw a Black person who played the cello." I would take a long way home to avoid the kids so they couldn't tease me. Dad didn't push any of us to continue playing our instruments once we lost interest. I think he realized that we weren't musically talented children. We did not have ambitions of playing in a symphony orchestra.

Dad loved music, especially jazz, classical, and rhythm and blues. He played gospel music as well. He bought lots of records and tapes. He listened to music at home and in the car on our long trips. He told me that music was an exercise for the brain. He massaged our brains with the music he enjoyed. We were not allowed to listen to soul and pop music at all. Leroy and I would sneak a radio into the bedroom and turn it down low to listen to the Soul Music channel.

On Saturdays, the famous TV show *Soul Train* came on. Dad didn't allow us to watch it, but mom would let us watch when he wasn't home. She said it reminded her of the experiences attending dances in the Black community where she grew up. Mom would show us some of the dances she used to do, like "The Jerk" and the "Watusi." I wanted to learn how to dance as they did on *Soul Train*. I would practice in the bathroom with the door locked, watching my awkward gyrations in private. *Soul Train* gave me a visual representation of Black culture, and I was in awe of it.

When I was younger, I watched soap operas with my mom every day. I learned how White people loved, cheated, argued, and sought money and fame. My favorite TV shows were *Leave it to Beaver* and *Mayberry R.F.D.* I loved the small-town country home life portrayed in those shows. I learned how White people treated those they loved and respected. I observed the ways that they valued their family and community heritage and traditions. When there was conflict or community unrest, they called town meetings and figured it out together. On the show "Leave It to Beaver," Eddie Haskell bullied Beaver and other kids in the neighborhood. I noticed that he was corrected and given consequences in a restorative way instead of just being punished. I learned later in life that Black people received different treatment when they misbehaved.

Mom and I watched every beauty queen contest, which taught me how the world set the standard of beauty for a White woman. I knew I wasn't up to that standard, but I longed to be a queen, adorned with a sparkly crown and dressed in a fabulous designer gown made just for me, draped in a red robe. I also loved watching comedy shows like *The Dick Van Dyke Show* and *The Carol Burnett Show*. I learned to love White humor in these shows. The characters filled my heart with laughter.

I believed in the "white picket fence" American Dream. I began to realize that our family shared many of the same moral values as these TV families did. Dad taught us to believe in and respect humanity. I also watched classic movies and Broadway musicals. I adored the high fashion outfits they wore with confidence and grace. From their hairstyle to their matching hat, every woman had a polished look, gloves, with coats or minks draped around their narrow backs and shoulders. I enjoyed the showgirls as they executed dance choreography across the beautifully designed backdrops on Broadway stages. Most of all, I was in awe of the romantic love stories. I equated true love to White love. White love was the ultimate model that the world had to follow to live happily ever after.

I was a Black girl looking through White eyes. It made me angry that White people didn't see me as the person I was striving to be. I longed to feel beautiful and to be accepted by society. Instead, I was facing difficulties living as a Black girl. I was searching for my own identity, and my mother was my only accessible role model. I know my parents must have seen the disparity between what they honored about our Black culture and what they knew I was missing in the Black experience.

Friends In Black

Dad took us to a few COGIC churches in San Diego before he decided to join one of the largest Black churches in the city. Jackson Memorial Church of God In Christ was under the leadership of Bishop J.A. Blake Sr. My siblings and I were so excited! The church was full of Black youth, and it was my only social experience with Black people throughout the week. There were choirs and youth ministries that included children's groups to young adults' groups. Mom quickly became involved in the women's ministry and vacation bible school. She also got involved with the music ministry. After a while, she became a choir president. Dad was instrumental in starting the audiovisual ministry at the church. He filmed and recorded Sunday morning services. It was a church on the move, and we were the new kids on the block.

Our initial induction to the Black youth Christian culture was rocky. The other kids called us the proper-talking McGee kids. I was even called an Oreo. It was the first time I experienced prejudicial treatment from other Black people. I couldn't believe how much I felt the other Black kids at church disliked me, especially the girls. I looked and acted differently than the

White El
Cajon

kids in Southeast San Diego who attended the church. They all had long-term relationships and generational connections with each other. They went to neighborhood schools and played sports or were in extracurricular activities together. We were known as the family that lived in White El Cajon. Beyond the church, we had no connection with any of them.

My brother met and became friends with a boy named Jimmy. Jimmy had Black swag. He wore a big afro that resembled the Black character Link for the 1970's TV series *Mod Squad.* He talked with confident articulation. He had a great sense of humor and loved to challenge anyone's thinking. Jimmy accepted us with open arms, despite how others may have felt about us. He was the leader and spokesperson of the other Black teens at church during that time. Jimmy got along with just about everyone. He had his own identity and a style that gave pause and drew attention to his presence. My brother and Jimmy hit it off the moment they met. I believe Jimmy was just curious enough to delve deeply into the McGee culture. He knew from the start that we were special. Our differences made for good conversation and new experiences. There were other boys named Joey, Rodney, and Michael, who followed Jimmy into a friendship with my brother. The four boys became affectionately known as the "Jackson Memorial Gang." They became fond of hanging out with our family. A couple of them had alternative motives--they were interested in my sister Esther and me. I became extremely close to Jimmy because of his personality. He was able to hold me captive in conversations that ranged from the simplest to the most profound subjects.

One Christmas, the Jackson Memorial Gang all got new bikes. They decided to ride from San Diego to El Cajon to visit with my brother. We were so excited. It was the first time we had all Black friends over our house. Dad and mom welcomed them with snacks and drinks. Of course, Esther and I found our way into the middle of the gang. We were trying to stoke the interest we knew a couple of them had in us. Mom was never too far away from the group of teens. The Jackson Memorial Gang all loved my mom. She was fun and made them feel welcome to come over anytime. Dad kept his distance but would make his presence known just long enough to command the respect he felt was due to him. By allowing the Jackson Memorial Gang to visit, Mom and dad provided what they knew we had been missing in our lives--Black friendships.

Sounds like Justo

A New Language

As my siblings and I were becoming comfortable and happy to be around Black friends, our world began to open up. I felt like I was finally Black looking through Black eyes. I could see a part of me that had been missing throughout my early childhood. I wanted to dress differently, talk differently and be different. One day, I went into the bathroom to practice speaking Black. I heard Ebonics slide off the teenager's lips and watched the roll of their necks at church. I wanted to talk and jester in the same way. Mom heard me in the bathroom working hard at my new language. She quickly called me out of the bathroom and sat me down to talk. She was concerned that I was trying to be someone else. Mom reminded me that no matter how much I tried to practice being or acting like someone other than myself, it would only be pretending.

"That's just not what God intended you to be," she said. "No matter what, people just have to accept you as you are, and if they can't, then it's their loss and not yours." I've carried that conversation in my bag all these years of my journey. If someone isn't willing to accept me, it's their loss.

The girls at the church didn't take to liking me. In the beginning, they never showed interest in getting to know my sister and me. Esther and I were teased and laughed at constantly. We didn't have that "Black girl from East San Diego" attitude. Esther and I had our own identity, and these other girls just didn't like it. Every time they came around us, they would speak "Pig Latin," a language used in Black culture that moves the first consonant or consonant cluster to the end of a word. It was foreign to us. We couldn't figure it out fast enough to speak it or understand what they were saying about us. No one was willing to teach it to us. It infuriated my sister and me! So, we made up our own language called "Ah-key." I won't give away our secret as to how we speak it. We worked long and hard perfecting it. Soon, when the church girls started speaking Pig Latin in front of us, Esther and I would Ah-key, leaving them looking quite puzzled.

I wanted to get along with the girls, but most of them would not stray in my direction. There were the ringleaders--the Harvey girls. They were a large family of sisters who earned the badge of rabble-rousers at church. One day, I got in a physical fight with one of them, named Leona, because she attempted to slap Baby Sister. Leona and I exchanged punches, pulled hair, kicked, and ripped at each other's clothes. We fought until someone separated us and quickly ushered both of us straight to the altar. I suddenly realized that I had gotten into my first fight with someone who was Black. I had a flashback thinking about the church fight my family had witnessed years before in Buffalo, New York. I thought dad was going to leave this church like he had left that one.

The church Bishop chastised Leona and me. He made us forgive one another in front of the whole church. We did apologize, but it meant nothing to me. It didn't resolve the anger I had toward Leona for trying to hurt my sister. My dad never punished me or chastised me about the fight. He only asked if I hit her first. I explained that I had fought her in Baby Sister's defense.

"Always protect your sisters," he said. "It's your responsibility never to let anyone hurt them, especially if you are the only one around to protect them."

Privately, Mom added, "Next time, if there is a next time, do it again. Never fear anyone! I am proud of you."

From that moment on, I felt like The Harvey's and the McGee's were like the Hatfield's and the McCoy's! However, because our common ground was at church, our contempt for each other never escalated beyond an eye roll, and a few mean words mumbled toward each other. We remained enemies until they left the church.

How sad.

A Friend for Life

I met Meredith, my friend for life, at church. She was my first Black female friend. She was a year younger than me, but she acted a lot older. One day, as I entered the women's lounge at the church, Meredith was sitting there in a multicolored patterned dress that matched the fashion flair of the 1940s. It was one of my favorite eras of women's fashion. When she stood up to go to the mirror to adjust her belt, the full skirt attached to the bodice of the dress moved in a swaying motion. She stood tall and confident.

"Hi," she said gently.

I was shocked that she even spoke to me; none of the other girls ever did. After a few seconds, I returned her kindness.

"Hello," I replied.

I watched Meredith apply powder to her face in a sophisticated way. She looked like Natalie Cole to me. She exemplified class, modestly adorning her shapely figure. She always wore 1940s jewelry--rings, bracelets, and necklaces filled with colorful jewels and rhinestones. She certainly dressed much older than she was. Her laughter was joyful, and her sense of humor was fun. She didn't hang around the other girls and never acted like them. Once we began to learn more about each other, we felt we were kindred spirits. I didn't know that mom and dad had already connected with Meredith's parents. Her dad, Elder Eddings, and my dad were in the military and very like-minded. Ruby Eddings, Meredith's mother, and my mom shared similar stories of being military wives. Meredith had six siblings.

113

Our two families shared many unforgettable times. My dad bought a motorhome and used it to drive the family to church in San Diego on the weekends. Dad didn't want to go back to El Cajon once we left to attend church Sunday mornings. So, after the Sunday morning service, dad would take us to the beach in the motorhome. Mom would cook our Sunday dinner while we enjoyed ourselves outside. After dinner, we cleaned up and prepared to go back to church for Young People's Willing Workers and then evening service. We stayed in church all day long on Sundays. We returned on Tuesdays for choir rehearsals, on Wednesdays for bible study, and on Fridays for youth church. There just weren't enough days in the week to serve the Lord! Soon after Dad bought our motorhome, Elder Eddings purchased one too. Our families did everything together, from weekend trips to the desert to Sundays at the beach to visiting my Aunt Marie and her family who lived in Texas. Now we were known as the Eddings and the McGees.

Meredith and I became extremely close. Her family lived in a two-story home, and her bedroom was at the corner of the second floor. I enjoyed going to her house on Sundays when we didn't go to the beach. Her mother would cook delicious dinners. My mom would sit and talk to Ruby for hours. Dad and Elder Eddings would do the same. Ruby had a contagious laugh that rang out from her belly. She was physical when she relished in laughter. Ruby would grab, rock, and slap through the laughter until she felt content and it subsided. I knew Mom was a dear friend of Ruby's because she would let her rock her body and slap her shoulder with joy the whole time while we visited. *What a blessing CB*

I loved going upstairs to Meredith's room. She had an antique vanity dresser with a matching chair she would pull up to the mirror. She stayed in that mirror. On her dresser, she had about 30 tiny perfume samples. I never saw a whole bottle of perfume there. She'd comb her hair back into a ponytail and pin on a hairpiece. Put on her makeup and then pick out one of her sample perfumes as if it were a full bottle and dab it on her wrist and her neck. Then she'd grab some lotion and massage it into her hands and arms until she felt satisfied. I asked so many questions about her samples. She must have felt sorry for me because she gave me a few perfume samples to take home with me.

I learned a lot from Meredith. She taught me how to appreciate the simple things and make them seem larger than life itself. She set her own path. She is genuine, and our friendship is uniquely powerful. She always permitted me to be myself. She didn't judge me for being different, which confirmed that we had the same heart and would be friends for life. Soon after we graduated, Meredith left for the military. We lost contact for many years, but I knew we would reconnect one day. I wasn't going to let the same thing happen to our friendship as it did with Becky, my long-lost friend from Morro Bay.

Cultural Self-Love

Dad and mom gave me a gift of cultural self-love. They engaged me in a church with a good youth ministry. They let me have personal interactions with our friends at church and home. They also supported me in working through my struggle to find comfort in my Blackness. Our friends from church, especially Jimmy and Meredith, showed me how similar we were even though we were raised and lived in completely different neighborhoods. They showed me the essence of Black pride during a time in my life when I struggled to know how to exercise it.

Interesting

By the time my brother and I were in High School together in 1972, some San Diego school districts acknowledged Martin Luther King's Birthday as a school holiday. Our school district didn't recognize MLK Jr. Day yet. So, the Jackson Memorial Gang decided to catch the bus out to our school to protest in support of equal rights. We were determined to use our voices to get the day off in honor of Dr. King. My brother and I were the only Black students in our school at the time. When the four Jackson Memorial Gang members showed up, there were suddenly more Black kids on campus than ever before. Mom was supportive; she made it known to the school administration that the district should make MLK Jr. Day a holiday. Later, dad drove the Jackson Memorial Gang home. I was so proud to be Black that day. I was also proud that my parents supported us.

Chicken Fried Hate

Growing up, I didn't have any White friends over our house. I met a White friend named Lynn in High School. She sat in front of me and would flip her long, light brown hair behind her back, where it would land on the top of my desk. I would throw it back across her shoulder. That's how we became friends. One day, I asked my parents if Lynn could come over. They gave permission, so I started hanging out with Lynn more. Finally, she asked me if I wanted to go to her house for dinner. I asked my parents, and they said yes.

Once I arrived, Lynn's mother greeted me at the door. She was extremely frail, barely standing five feet, three inches tall. She immediately began rambling about how excited she was to have me as a dinner guest. Lynn's mother escorted me to the table. It was set to serve dinner to six people, including Lynn's father and two siblings.

"Can you find which seat I picked out for you?" Lynn's mother asked.

I pointed to a random seat; I was wrong.

"No. Tonight I prepared fried chicken for dinner because you were coming. I know Black people eat chicken with their hands. So, you will sit at the place setting without silverware," she said. Then, she added, "To make it easier, I'm giving you the drumstick. The rest of us will be eating breasts and thighs."

I burned with anger. I quickly thought of how my dad would want me to respond to her disrespect.

"May I please have silverware at my place setting as well?" I managed to ask politely.

Lynn's mother reluctantly placed a knife and fork at the empty place setting.

I had never eaten fried chicken with a knife and fork, but I wanted to prove Lynn's mother wrong. Before I began to tackle my drumstick, I shot Lynn a look of cold-hearted hatred across the table. Then I started chasing my chicken with my knife and fork while longing to be back in the presence of my parents. I pushed peas and mashed potatoes off the sides of my plate, making a mess like a child. I quickly moved what I could back onto my plate. After a few embarrassing moments, I had skinned the drumstick to the bone. I asked permission to be excused from my seat and use the phone to call my parents to pick me up.

When my parents arrived, I got in the car and screamed out as loud as I could, "I hate Lynn! Her parents are prejudiced. She knew it before she invited me over for dinner."

I explained to my parents what happened with immense anger. I cried profusely, trying to catch my breath in between each sentence. My mother wanted to go back to the house and tell Lynn's mother a thing or two. Dad said, "You handled it just the way I would've expected you to. I am proud of you for not disrespecting an adult. That's how you maturely handle things."

I knew that was what dad would say, but that wasn't what I wanted to hear. I wanted dad to be as mad as mom and me. I wanted him to give me permission to tear into Lynn at school the next day. I wanted to hurt her physically to match the hurt I was feeling emotionally. I didn't know what to do with my anger. My parents told me that they understood my pain, but I didn't believe them. I thought they would never understand my pain because they weren't there with me. No one was there with me, not even Lynn. I sat in my anger. I didn't want to let go of it.

I didn't speak to Lynn for months. She finally wrote me a letter stating that both of her parents were alcoholics. It said that her mother had been drunk, and she made a fool of the family that night with her ignorance about Black culture. I had no experience with the effects of alcoholism; my parents didn't drink. Lynn's letter went on to say that she would give anything and do anything to remain friends with me. She wrote how much she wished she had parents like mine. She never heard arguing, cussing, disrespectful comments from my family. She said she was at peace when she would come over to my house. I forgave Lynn and felt sorry that she had to live in an environment like that at home. Lynn and I remained friends throughout high school. She taught me how to drive a stick shift. To this day, every time I drive a stick shift, I think about her. Soon after high school, she got married and moved away. I went to visit her once in Arizona. Her parents had passed away. I never got a chance to restore my relationship with them. Lynn was different at that time, and so was I. We had grown up and apart. I didn't contact her again after that visit.

This fried chicken story has stayed with me and reminds me of how assumptions and ignorance can tear human relationships apart. Hurt and harm exist in intentional and unintentional ways. Time will pass without restoring broken relationships if you let it. I did. Years later, I was asked to speak to teachers and administrators about my experience being the only Black girl in high school. They wondered how I had handled it. I explained how my parent's love and guidance helped get me through the tough times. Then, I shared the Fried Chicken story. I began to weep while sharing it with these educators; it was still hurtful. I know I will never forget the experience. It taught me how to appreciate the Christian home I grew up in and follow my parents' example. It was crucial for me to unpack those dark moments in my life. Otherwise, I could have carried hatred in my heart forever.

Black Confidence

As a young Black girl, I went through high school with a new attitude of who I was becoming. I took liberty at letting anyone know I was not going to be talked down to or called out of my name. I got into several fights. Every time they issued me a referral and called my parents, mom and dad would come to the school to support me.

I had several mini-altercations in the hallway or the PE locker room. I remember the rage I felt when I was getting dressed for PE. All the White girls would watch me undress. When I asked a White girl what she was looking at, she dared to call me "Black nigger bitch." This girl badgered me every day. When I couldn't ignore it anymore, I fought her in the back of the school next to the football field. My PE teacher saw me fighting and made me go to the office with her. She told me that she was disappointed with me and that I should have told a teacher what the girl was doing to me. I knew it wouldn't matter if I told any adult on that campus. They probably would have taken the girl's side, just as this teacher was doing. When I got to the office, the principal called my dad. When Dad arrived, he listened to what happened. Then, in front of the Vice-Principal, he said, "Cynthia, it is time for you to stop being so aggressive and learn how to be more assertive. People will respect you more in the long run."

"What does assertive mean?" I asked him. He told me to look it up when we got home. I learned that assertive meant *"having or showing a confident personality."* A bit much

That day in 10th grade, I began changing how I responded to someone who tried to challenge my self-confidence. I liked gaining respect by the way I carried myself and how I chose to speak my truth. I was energized to accomplish my goals because of my confidence in who I was and my abilities. Dad taught me that being a McGee was more than just a name. There were intentional actions I needed to take to manage the responsibility of being a McGee. Now I was coming full circle from understanding being Black to being confident in my Black being. Now I move at an assertive pace in my life's journey, carrying my Black travel bag. I always make sure to remain in lockstep with my faith to lead in a way that others will want to follow.

EXTENSION OF LOVE

Extended Family

Throughout my life I didn't get the opportunity to experience spending time getting to know my extended family on either my mother's or father's side to a great extent. Even though my father's parents passed away when he was a young boy, I never met his brothers and sisters until the sister who raised him passed away when I was around 11 years old. Her name was Lueticher, affectionately known as "LC." Dad loved her dearly. He drove the whole family to her funeral services in Ohio. When we arrived, dad dropped my siblings and I off at this tan colored house with a lot of people inside. I only remember meeting one of his brothers, Uncle Curtis. Dad was the youngest out of six siblings. He had two brothers, and three sisters. I remember hearing the name of his youngest sister, Aunt Mary, but can't remember actually having words with her. My siblings and I didn't go to the funeral. We stayed at that house for hours before dad and mom came back to pick us up. It was nighttime when we left. Dad drove back to his Aunt LC's house where he was raised. He got out of the car and made his way into the empty house. I followed him. He walked slowly through a couple of rooms and then into the kitchen, never saying a word. It was as if he was experiencing a slow-motion flashback over his life growing up there as a child. Then he made an abrupt stop at the refrigerator. He threw his arm over the top and dropped his head into the crease of his elbow. I stood silently by his side. Like the quiet before the storm, he let out a painful moan swelling into a bellowing cry. Then in a whisper, he said, "Thank you." Dad pulled out a white handkerchief, wiped his eyes, and blew his nose. He tucked the handkerchief in his pocket then walked soberly outside looking toward the night sky. With tears in my eyes, I grabbed his hand, hoping that feeling my presence would let him know I was there for him. He never acknowledged me, but I knew he knew my intention. I was honored to witness that moment with my dad. I had never seen him cry or express his emotions until that day. It didn't happen again until I was in my late 50's. He was a man who carried the weight of his life on his shoulders, never asking for help, even if it became too much for him to bear. However, in that moment, I knew God gave my dad the strength to push through a tremendous level of grief, pain, and sorrow. Dad was strong in his way of thinking and being. The military trained him well in exercising mental strength. He transferred it to his family with ease. When things seemed tough for him, he loved to say, "I'm an Airman!" Once he said that I had all the confidence in the world that he and everything else would be ok. Dad never invited his family from Ohio or Mississippi to visit us. We never had personal relationships with anyone on my dad's side. We only knew of them by name. He felt strongly about not having his children around his type of family. He basically felt the same way about my mom's family. We were never allowed to spend the long summer breaks or holidays with any of our extended family members. *Some of family is SAD*

Could have been a testimony I did to my kids

Mary Frances

We didn't get a chance to know our grandparents because both sets of them either passed away before we were born or while we were young. However, dad had a favorite niece. They were raised together. She was the only one who dad personally invited into our home. She and her husband Blaine, who lived in Oakland, CA drove down to see my dad during my high school years. In fact, one time we had the privilege of having Thanksgiving dinner with her and her husband. Well after I graduated from high school, during a holiday season, I went with my dad, Mary Frances and her husband Blaine to a Christmas musical called "The Colors of Christmas" in San Francisco. I dressed up in a beautiful black pantsuit. For the first time, I was having a daddy-daughter night out. It was magical. The musical was amazing! The whole time I was there, I thought about my sisters and wanted them to have the same experience. I compelled my dad to promise to invite them to see it the following year. He made good his promise; the next year he bought tickets for my sisters and sister-in-law to see

"The Colors of Christmas" in the City of Cerritos. It was closer to San Diego. We had a wonderful time. Dad gave us a gift that night. I prayed it would happen again, and soon. But it didn't. The Colors of Christmas stopped performing after a few years. I gained a high level of respect for Mary Frances when I visited her with dad to see the musical. My respect for her remains to this day. She is an educated, professional woman. She is sophisticated and carries herself with confidence and grace. She speaks in a soft proper talking voice that reminds me of a storybook narrator who captivates my mind with the wonder of what she will read on the next page of the book. She is physically fit, and dresses semi-casually, comfortably transitioning from office wear to an outfit perfect for attending an afternoon lunch at a tennis or golf club. She is an excellent cook and I love to watch her navigate her way around the kitchen. She respects the benefit and value of healthy cooking with fresh market foods. She taught me about the ease of cooking with a non-stick cast iron skillet. She challenged my dad with respectful, common-sense thoughts and questions that left him speechless at times. She is extremely liberal; dad was extremely conservative. Their conversations were quite entertaining. Her love for my dad was genuine and deeply rooted. While dad and I were visiting Mary Frances, I noticed the warm relationship dad had with her as his niece. They laughed and teased each other, talked about their likes, dislikes, aspirations, and accomplishments. They relished in one another's company for hours, with conversations running late into the night. Watching their interaction, I learned that dad highly respected a woman who could stand toe to toe to him, with independent, intellectual thinking. Mary Frances did that well! I took note and packed it away in my bag of essentials saving it for an opportunity to do the same with dad, and any other man like him.

Aunt Marie

Before I graduated my mother's younger sister, Aunt Marie came to visit my mom with her children. I affectionately call her Marie. This was a treat for us because we never had cousins come to our house to visit while we were growing up. My Aunt Marie loves my mother beyond expression. The love she had for my mom completely solidifies the definition of sisterly love. Their feelings may have been expressed differently at times, but the love was evident. I knew my mom would give her sister anything she had and then some. Aunt Marie has a fun personality. She loves shoes and dressing up in beautiful suits and hats for church. As a First Lady of the church, she is highly respected. She stands a little under 5'4" tall, with a medium-size body frame. Over the years her hair has become a beautiful silver tone color that outshines and puts any other shade of gray hair to shame. Marie is my favorite aunt. She has always made me feel special ever since I was a kid. Our conversations, moments of laughter together are memorable. I treasure the private moments we've cried together during her moments of tragedy, as moments that deepened our relationship and love for one another. She loves to eat almost more than I do. We have shared some incredible times together over food. While she was visiting us, Marie's sweet tooth stumbled upon some name-brand cinnamon rolls. She couldn't wait to tell me about them. Once I got home from school, she asked me to go with her to the store to get some more. On the way there she described the rolls in such a detailed way that I could hardly wait to taste them. We got the cinnamon rolls, drove to a mall, and sat down on a bench. Our goal was to go shopping with mom after we ate the rolls. Before we could get comfortable on the bench, she went through a short ritual, ensuring that I would enjoy the taste to the fullest. She opened the package with care, gently tore one roll apart from the others, and then broke off another piece. Then, she slowly folded the buttery sweet bread swirled with cinnamon and slathered with buttercream icing into her mouth which hung open in anticipation of it reaching her molars to begin the delicious burst of goodness. I sat there in awe as I watched her enjoy that cinnamon roll. She moaned and groaned, threw her hands, surrendering like she was being held hostage to the taste. She chewed a few times before she finally swallowed it. She rocked her head from side to side, then gathered herself.

"Oh Cynthia, now you gotta taste it," she said. I released a loud, gut-wrenching laughter from the core of my being.

"Marie, is it really that good?" I asked.

"YES GURL!" she said, looking me straight into my eyes without flinching. With that, I went for it. Following every move that she had made, I got the cinnamon roll out of the package and into my mouth. It was amazingly delicious! Believe me, we sat there and ate almost the whole package, laughing as we enjoyed each caloric morsel, along with the joy of being in the company of each other. That has been the best cinnamon roll experience in my whole life. I can taste it now. I complimented her on how well she made food seem to taste just by watching her eat. In return, she told me that every time I eat French fries, she would want some of her own because of the way I ate them. I never put the whole fry in my mouth at one time. I always eat one half of the fry at a time, before following through finishing the second half. Only Marie would notice something as simple as the way I eat my French fries.

Marie and mom shopped a lot together, they would hang out in the malls, Sears, Macy's department stores, fabric stores all day. I would tag along, watching them would put items in their shopping cart, and sometimes take items out. Then when they reached the counter, they would tell the cashier, "I think I'm gonna wait on this," and then walk away. Then they would head off to the next store to do the same until they found a treasure that they couldn't leave the store without. After a full day of shopping, they would go eat ice cream together, sitting and laughing for as long as their hearts desired. Mom loved recounting her childhood stories, from her school years, to the day she met my dad. One of Marie's favorite stories was when mom got in a fight at school with a girl who was bullying her. Mom had her on the ground beating her up in a winning fashion. Marie described how all of a sudden, the girl asked mom to let her up to take her watch off. Mom ceased fighting and let her get up. Before mom knew it, she was on the ground and the girl was on top now, beating the mess out of her. Unfortunately, mom lost that fight. Marie laughs every time she tells the story and always ends saying, "Eddie Mae I don't know why you let that girl trick you by letting her get up. You were winning the fight!" Then she, mom, and I would laugh together about that memory.

Marie loved and respected my dad. She called him Willie and sometimes just "McGee". Dad was like a big brother to Marie. She admits to this day that dad was the best brother-in-law, and that mom was the best sister she had. Dad knew how much my mom loved her sister and tried to honor their relationship as much as possible. He kept an open invitation for Marie to visit my mom whenever she wanted. As Marie grew older dad would offer her advice that she respects to this day. When she decided to marry a man named Bishop Williams, Marie asked dad to give her away. My mom and dad drove to Denver where Marie lived at the time for the wedding. Dad was honored to give her away and Marie was proud to have my dad at her side on her wedding day. Her husband promised Marie that he would take her to see her sister in California as often as he could, and he did. We eventually saw Marie a lot more when Bishop Williams and my aunt moved to Moreno Valley. He had family in Los Angeles. San Diego was the perfect distance for both of them to visit their families. Marie loved California, she called it her "paradise." Our extended family grew when her son, my cousin Frank, who we call "Bull", moved his family of six children and his wife Dianne to El Cajon. They lived across the street from our family. Because we were so used to living life with just our core family members oftentimes holidays and personal celebrations were void of their presence in our home. It was different having cousins our same age living in the same town. We didn't exercise the freedom of showing up at our cousin's house unannounced. We were taught that it was improper and disrespectful to do so. We needed to call before just showing up at anyone's door, even family. We would go months without seeing one another. But we didn't feel like we were missing out on family time because we had gone years without having the luxury of spending time with our cousins. Bull and his oldest daughter Lisa, called Peaches, showed their love for us by intentionally reaching out to my siblings and me. They connected more to Leroy and me, because we were the oldest. We got to know them as family members and shared some great times together. Bull is my favorite cousin growing up. He treats me more like a sister at times and never forgets to call just to tell me he loves me. He is full of love and has a heart packed with kindness. He is the hardest worker I know. In fact, he loves to work to a fault! Bull was always athletic. He refuses to believe that he is as old as he is in his mind. Instead, he allows his heart to believe that he is as young as he feels and looks.

Peaches is Bull's oldest daughter. She fulfills the same caretaker role in her family as I do in mine. She is responsible and a hard worker like her father. She is ambitious. She does as much as she can for her siblings without asking permission. When necessary, she doesn't mind asking for forgiveness later. Before she married her wonderful husband Jason, she let nothing stand in the way of her exploring life to the fullest. Peaches and I have shared some deep conversations about her faith, especially when life became difficult for her. She has always respected my advice.

Finally, my Aunt Linda Jean, who is a jewel in the family. Linda Jean is intellectually disabled. She came to live with our family in the early 1970s. She has a kind spirit until you get her upset. Then she shows the fiery side of her personality. Linda Jean carries herself in a quiet manner. She is socially appropriate and independently cares for herself on a daily basis. Living with Linda Jean gave me the insight that I needed to understand the complexities, patience, and sensitivity a family should have when sharing space in your life with a disabled person. I feel privileged to have a special relationship with her. These extended family members shared time with our family. They taught me the value and appreciation of connecting to an extension of my parents and not just the core of our nuclear McGee family. My sister Esther gave us a gift of learning more about my dad's lineage. Over the years has shared some intriguing facts about his incredible history. My Aunt Marie shared stories about my mother's lineage as well. I'm thankful for both of their contributions to my knowledge about my parents.

Family Traditions

Our family traditions were special in our household. Thanksgiving and Christmas were my mom's favorite holidays. In fact, all of us lived for these holidays to share beautiful times together. It was just our family of six growing up and we didn't care about anyone else's experience because no one else

CB You were blessed to live a white life... I got it now

mattered to us. Mom would begin cooking the night before Thanksgiving and Christmas. She stayed up literally all night long baking her famous pecan tarts, sweet potato pies, and white cake--her dad's favorite. Her cornbread dressing was a classic southern staple for the dinners. She made homemade potatoes with snap green beans and homemade dinner rolls. She basted the turkey around 5:00 a.m. so that it would be done right after 1:00 pm, just in time for dad to carve it so we were ready to eat around 2:00 pm. My sisters and I assisted mom all night long. We prepped, chopped, rolled dough, peeled potatoes and so much more. It was the best time of my life experiencing Jazz music and Christmas music playing with a crackling fire burning all night in the living room fireplace. We would throw our blankets and pillows across the floor to catch a nap in between taking turns assisting mom. She never sat down at all. She worked all night without a break making sure everything was perfectly timed to be on the table Thanksgiving and Christmas afternoon. After the table was set, we would all rush back to our rooms to change into our new holiday outfits. Then dad would turn on the video camera and film us coming down the hallway to model them. It was the corniest moment, but we all laughed and enjoyed doing it so much. We dressed up for each other as if we were invited guests in our own home. The most treasured specialty and family tradition is McGee Tea! It is a sweet tea with a bubbly twist. It is our non-alcoholic drug of choice drink that no one can get enough of. Once it hits your saliva glands it stimulates an incredibly delicious taste that causes an addictive sugar high that keeps you coming for it all day and night. In fact, we were hooked on it the whole holiday season!

Between the lack of sleep, overdosing on McGee Tea, and binging on mom's food for three days straight, our laughter and love of being around each other is a feeling matched to none. No fussing, no cussing, no discontent, no yelling, no substance or alcohol intake interfered with our ability to experience pure fun. I always provided the games to play each year; Monopoly was a constant. Our family entertained ourselves and loved each other in a genuine way. Once more the love and synergy of my family was at its best; I never wanted it to end.

High School Years

Dad required us only to make As and Bs in school. C grades were not acceptable, especially once we reached high school. Dad paid us money for every A and B on our report cards. We got nothing for a C. One time I got a D in math on my report card. I was terrified to confront my dad about my inability to earn a better grade. I didn't want to face the shame of being compared to my siblings. I knew I was going to get the least amount of money for my report card that day. I had cheer practice after school, so dad was already home from work when I arrived at the house. I stood nervously at the front door for a while, working up the courage to face the inevitable. I prayed to God that He let the confrontation pass quickly. I was convinced that it wasn't my fault; I had tried as hard as I could.

I walked in and saw dad. My whole body trembled as I handed him the report card without him asking for it. He shook his head in disappointment.

That's WRONG

I feel

"This D subtracts the money you would have gotten for the A's and B's," he said sternly. He handed back my report card, turned, and walked away. I stood there, without any money, hanging my head in shameful sorrow.

I Know this

Math is my intellectual challenge. It's the one subject I tried to avoid throughout my educational career. Teachers are influential and can use that power in positive as well as detrimental ways. In 9th grade, I had a math teacher who was incredibly mean, impatient, and prejudiced. I had math as my first-period class. I am not a morning person at all, and so my brain was slow to process math so early in the day. One day, I came to class a few minutes late. I gave my teacher my late pass. Before I could get settled into my seat, he asked me to answer a homework assignment question. The math problem involved converting fractions to decimals--a process I struggled with in math. I scrambled to get out my homework paper, then gave him the answer I had. He wrote my answer out in huge figures on the green chalkboard.

We have much in common

"Ok," he said. "Where should the decimal be?" I had no idea!

"Umm, on the bottom," I answered. The teacher bent down and drew a large white dot on the floor. As he did so, the entire class burst out in laughter, mocking and pointing at me while I shrank in my seat.

Mr Molshanock

"Is this what you mean?" He replied. I never answered him.

He put the decimal in the right place on the board, never explaining to me why it belonged there. I decided that day I hated math with a passion and that it also hated me. I vowed never to answer a math problem in front of a class again; I never have since that day.

A FEW PRECIOUS LETTERS MOM WROTE
ME DURING MY HIGH SCHOOL YEARS

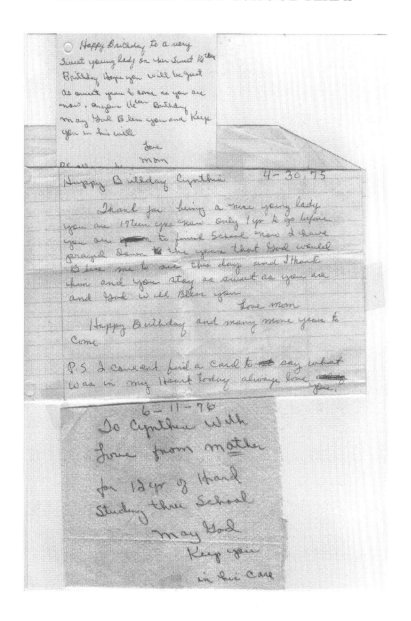

My First Real Job

My high school years went by fast. I really didn't like anything about the school except our top-rated football team, cheering for my brother, and working as a TA in the special education department. I didn't get any special recognitions or acknowledgment for what I accomplished in school. I just wanted to graduate and get on with my life. I was in the 11th grade when I finally got a real job outside of babysitting. I had turned 16 and gotten my driver's license. I was delivering flowers at a nearby florist shop. I had to drive a big white van with wooden racks across the back of the van with holes in them that held the flower arrangements. I was super excited about working. I felt independent and responsible. There was a clothing store right next to the flower shop. When I got paid, I would go directly to that store to shop. I spent my money as fast as I was making it. I had to learn how to budget a little more. One day, I had to deliver some flowers to a town called Lakeside. It was known as a town that Black people should not visit during those days. The house I was delivering to was on a dirt road off the beaten path. When I arrived, I was greeted by a man who was very angry.

"What the hell are you doing on my property?" he demanded.

I tried explaining to him that I was delivering flowers. He told me he didn't want any flowers from a nigger and that I was on private property. Thinking it might calm him down, I told him that the flowers were not from me but from someone who wanted to appreciate a person at this address. He replied I don't care! You touched the damn flowers right, therefore I don't

138

want anything coming from your hands to mine! Now get off my property." I was so afraid. I couldn't get that van off his property fast enough. Then I became angry. I couldn't wait to get back to the shop to tell my boss. By the time I arrived he had already gotten a call from that man demanding that they not send anyone Black to deliver flowers to his property again. Instead of supporting my right to continue working my job, my boss told me that it was too dangerous for me to continue delivering. He suggested that I start working in the shop as a helper to keep the shop clean and assist with making the arrangements. That's not what I was hired to do. I loved delivering.

"Why not just have two people deliver instead of me being by myself?" I asked.

"I can't afford to pay two people to deliver per shift," he said.

I quit the job after giving two weeks' notice. My parents both agreed it was best for me not to work there anymore if I was not happy with my new responsibilities. I was crushed and felt it was unfair for me to lose something I had worked so hard to get. Mom and dad told me if something is taken from you without cause, believe that there may be something better in store for you in return. Throughout my life, I realized that didn't mean I didn't have to work at getting something better. Quite frankly, I had to work harder. By living my life centered in the will of God and by following his biblical principles, I have received blessings and favor. At times I have been blown away with the abundance of blessings that were greater than any losses. Sometimes I didn't get the blessings I expected. However, I am blessed no matter what!

Heartbreaking Departure

Throughout his young manhood, Leroy pursued his dream of becoming a professional football player. My dad thought it was a waste of time, intellect, and physical energy. Dad always believed that a man should use his brain to make his way no matter how blessed he was with athletic talent. I always thought it was a strange thing for him to believe because dad liked watching sports. *Loss of the Blessing*

Leroy always admired dad, and dad was so proud to call Leroy his boy. However, you would hardly know the depth of their affection for each other by watching their relationship. They didn't spend a lot of quality time together, one on one. Leroy was much more of a Momma's Boy. Dad worked a lot and barely had time to hang out and play ball with Leroy. Dad spent quality time with my brother, teaching him all about technology and engineering. My brother picked up on everything dad taught him and did it well. It wasn't until later in life when the return on dad's investment with Leroy paid off. It was easier for my brother to please my mother than my dad. It was hard to impress dad with simple accomplishments in life. He always wanted us to be the best at everything, without any excuses. Leroy was the best at any sport he played, and yet it didn't seem to move dad's emotional Richter scale as much as it elated my mom and the rest of the family.

He was a hard man you CB

Carry much of that

140

cheerleader CB

I've watched my brother persevere through disappointments that would have shaken my world off its axis. Yet, his bounce-back allowed me to be a source of strength for him later in life that I never knew I could be. My brother would always tell my mom he was going to become a professional football player. He dreamed of buying her a red Corvette and a big house. I knew he wasn't going to stop until he made it come to fruition. I wanted to travel this journey with him. When he started playing football in high school, I had to wait two years to try out for varsity cheer to be on the field with him. I was overjoyed when I made the cheer squad.

My brother and I were the only Black students at the school we attended until my senior year. He was so good at football that they called him "Black Magic" on the field; they called me "Cindy--Leroy's sister," even though my name is Cynthia. At the time, being misnamed didn't matter to me. I was so proud for everyone to know I was "Leroy's sister." By this time, Leroy was the stud of the school and hung out with the other studs on campus. We weren't eating lunch together anymore. I was no longer saving my peanut butter and jelly sandwiches for him, but I was still giving him anything that I thought would make his day. When I got the opportunity to provide him with something, anything, I would call out "LEROY!" I would extend my hand, and he would take it from me in the hallway without stopping and thank me with a smile. *You needed him*

We are alike in this

I relished every moment I spent with my brother in high school in El Cajon. I cheered loud and hard for him. I ran up and down the football field, following him and celebrating with him

CB

Loving your brother

as he made touchdown after touchdown. It became the expectation in the commentator's booth as they announced." There goes Leroy McGee on a breakaway down the field...annnndddd his sister Cindy down the sideline into the end zone for another touchdown!" He was the best running back in the school's history during his years on the team and for years beyond his graduation. After Leroy graduated, he went on to play football for a local junior college for two years. I tried out for cheer while still in high school at the same college he was attending. I made the song squad and became the head song squad leader. When I graduated from high school, I couldn't wait to get on the football field alongside my brother. I couldn't believe how much my brother had grown up. He already looked like a professional football player.

Soon it was time to look for the four-year college where he wanted to play football. I knew most likely he wouldn't stay in our hometown and that he would be leaving to play at a school far away from home one day. When he announced that he got a scholarship to play for a big ten school in the Midwest, my heart dropped. I knew the months would pass by quickly before it would be time for him to leave. I planned for him the grandest going away party that my sister Esther and I held for him in our garage. It was so much fun! At the same time, I was slipping into a deep depression. My closest sibling, my hero, my play buddy, my fighting partner, my big brother Leroy was leaving me. I didn't know what I was going to do. When the day arrived for us to take him to the airport, I couldn't say a word. My throat felt like I had swallowed a mouth full of mothballs. I don't know how that feels, but I imagine it would feel like what I was experiencing at the time. The drive to the airport went by in a flash. I remember how sad I was and how hard it was for me to hold back my tears. He was so happy, and I didn't want to spoil his emotions. My whole family and a few friends sent him off to his new destination. I was so proud of his accomplishment. He had worked so hard for this moment. As he boarded the plane, he looked back and waved to everyone. I swore he was looking directly at me, telling me to be strong and to take care of the family while he is away. My eyes overflowed with tears. I couldn't keep them from rolling down my cheeks and under my chin. I tried, but they wouldn't stop at all. I couldn't breathe, and my heart hurt like someone was trying to dig it slowly out of my chest with a blunt object. I was frozen in those emotions for over a month.

When we arrived home from the airport, I fell face down on the living room couch and didn't want to leave that space. If I did, I would have to pass by Leroy's empty room, which was way too painful for me. Mom and dad let me stay in the living room for a few days. Then I was forced to get up and move past what I now know was one of the darkest depression episodes of my life at the time. After Leroy got settled in his new home in Michigan, he started writing to us and sharing his fun experiences at the college. I wrote and talked to him often over the phone. I prayed for him to stay strong and healthy to continue on his journey to the pros and buy my mom that red Corvette and big house one day.

MY FIRST POSTCARD FROM LEROY
AFTER HE LEFT FOR MICHIGAN AND A NOTE I
WROTE HIM FROM JUNIOR COLLEGE

Becoming My Own Woman

I finally graduated high school--without attending prom, because there was no one who wanted to take me to an all-White dance. Right after I graduated, dad retired from the Air Force. He gave the best of his life serving his country. It was a bitter-sweet moment for me because I really liked being an Air Force brat. I was sad knowing that I would miss dad dressing up in his military uniform every day. I knew we were done with long trips across the country. There would be no more

That's what you think of others. Much pride.

yellow and green Mayflower moving vans coming to help us relocate to our new destinations. Dad was officially a veteran, and we were now civilians. It felt like our social status had been lowered to that of the commonplace citizens. I proudly presented my military ID card to gain access to the bowling Alley, dance clubs, and the military annex on base. I would miss going to the commissary with mom most of all. However, I knew she would still shop for all our favorite foods at a cheaper cost. Soon after he retired, Dad was offered a job to help build Tracon, a control tower and tracking system, at Miramar military base. He was the first African American assigned to complete the four-year task. He traveled back and forth to Los Angeles every week because he refused to relocate our family again. He honored the fact that all of us were happy in our lives in school and work. It was time for him to respect the goals we had for our lives after we had supported his career in the Air Force. Dad promised that when he retired, we would live the normal lives we wanted.

Dad had strict expectations for us to live at home after graduating. We had to attend college, carry a full-time course load and get only A's and B's if we wanted to avoid the worry of paying for room and board. I didn't want to live at home under that kind of stress. I made up in my mind that I would move out as soon as I got a decent-paying job. I was horrible at math and stayed stressed out about trying to get at least a B in my math classes. In college, I took a deductive reasoning math class to fulfill my degree requirements. On the first day, I approached the instructor.

"What do I need to do to pass this class with a C?" I asked candidly.

"Why only a C?" he replied with a laugh.

"I am math-phobic, and I need this class to complete my degree. I've come too far not to achieve my aspirations," I answered.

My instructor gave me explicit instructions.

"Enroll in math tutoring. Attend class every day. Complete all of your homework. And no matter what, answer every problem on your tests."

"Deal," I said. "My only request is that you promise never to ask me to answer a problem in front of the class." He agreed.

I did everything he asked of me and passed the class with a grade of C+. I was elated that I never had to take another math class. I packed that experience of learning math in my bag. I still get anxious when I think of math, but now I reach for comfort in a simple pleasure--FRENCH FRIES!

Dad had started going to college in the evenings to earn his business degree. It seemed as if he was growing apart from the whole family as well as my mom. I talked privately to mom about my plan to move out. Our conversation quickly shifted to her sharing with me that she wished she would have taken time to live on her own before she got married to dad and started having children. She told me that I needed to be my own woman and learn how to take care of myself first before depending on a man to take care of me. She began to encourage

146

me to plan how I was going to let dad know that I was moving. Before I left, she wanted me to be as prepared as possible with the things I need to be ready to live in my own place. She told me I could take my bed and sheets with me when I moved. She started to get excited and wanted to go shopping with me to pick out things for my new place. She understood my reason for not wanting to go to college under the pressure of dad's rules. Mom wanted me to enjoy my learning experience. Once I had that talk with mom, my goal switched to a desire to make my mom proud of me by becoming an independent young woman. It was something she had missed out on doing for herself. I cleaned out my closet to make room for my new things for my apartment, even though I didn't know where I would be living. I needed a job badly and was applying all over while attending school. One day, a friend named Jackie called out my name as I was walking across campus "Cindy!" As I turned around, I caught her waving her hand and walking toward me. She asked me if I wanted a job. I thought it was strange for her to ask that out of the blue, but of course I said yes. She said her dad was a principal of a school in Kearny Mesa and is looking for a teacher's assistant. She said if I was interested, she would tell her dad. She gave me his phone number. When I got home, I called Mr. Lee and he set up an interview for me. I drove to the address he provided for me but quickly realized it was the wrong place. I was parked in front of Juvenile Hall Detention Facility. I went inside to call him to get the correct address. He chuckled and said I was at the right place. He asked the receptionist to buzz me in. After going through several buzzing doors, I walked into his office. I was in disbelief. "I thought you needed a TA." He said, "I do, for the school the boys go to during the daytime." I didn't know that when teens get locked up, they still have to go to school. He taught me about the educational laws and then interviewed me and took me on a tour around the facility. He called me the next day and offered me the job. I didn't know this would be the beginning of my professional journey; I hadn't even packed a bag for it.

After accepting the job, I found out that I had to be enrolled in school at least part-time in order to keep my position. It was an incentive to produce future educators from those of us who were working as TAs in the classrooms. I was about to experience a culture shock. My dad had always said that if he ever got a call from the police, he would tell them to keep us. This was the very place where I would have ended up if I had ever gotten in trouble with the law; now I was working there. I was curious as to how and why these kids were in Juvenile Hall. It seemed so unfair. I wondered whose fault it was. As I prepared for my first day of work, I also prepared to fill my closet up with the things I needed for my new home. I planned to be in it as soon as I saved up enough money to move out. I was ready for the world. The next thing I needed to do was have that talk with dad that mom told me to prepare to have. I reflected back on the mental notes of how Mary Frances communicated with my dad. I felt confident that I could do it as long as my plan made sense. I knew that Dad would challenge me because he always did. Leroy was getting ready to head off to Michigan State to play football. Our family was starting to look and feel different to me. I was sad, anxious and happy all at the same time. I didn't want to fail to meet my mom's expectation of me becoming an independent woman. I didn't want to meet my dad's expectations of living under his roof. For the first time in my life, I felt like my parents were on opposite sides of the fence based on what they wanted for me. I focused on fulfilling my mother's desire for my immediate future. I knew dad's desire for me would be fulfilled in the long run. He never wanted any of his children to forfeit achieving a higher education for unattainable aspirations or lofty dreams. I never questioned my ambition to live on my own or to accomplish what I aspired to be in life. I just needed to believe in both of them.

While I was still living at home, working and attending school, I left juvenile hall and moved to a different position at Hillcrest Receiving Home, a 24-hour care facility for court awarded children. I worked at the school there as a TA with a woman named Mary Ellen Reinhardt, also known as Whitney. Mary Ellen was an incredible teacher. She was a tall thin woman who always wore jeans with tennis shoes, a t-shirt with a Members Only jacket, and drove a Volkswagen van to work. She smiled with her eyes and was always happy and loved her job. She taught me how to connect with innocent children who had pain and tragedy in their lives that would bring me to tears. But after a moment or two of watching her magically touch the hearts of those children she would have them smiling, singing and holding onto her pant leg as if she was their biological parent. Mary Ellen taught me the secret of how to read Dr.

Seuss "Green Eggs and Ham" to a room full of children and hold them captive from the first page to the last. They would want to hear her read it over and over to them. I watched her become the characters in the book by bringing them to life. To this day, it is my favorite children's book. Mary Ellen solidified the reason why I wanted to become a teacher.

One day, Mary Ellen told me it was time for me to get my teaching degree. She felt I was ready for my own classroom. So, I decided to attend Mesa College to start my teaching degree program. My first semester I met my second friend for life, Trellis Patton. I was in a tennis class and about three tennis courts over, I heard a lady laughing hysterically alternating with my laughter on the first court. Oddly enough, the tennis instructor called both of us to a center court and said, "The two of you need to be partners. You're both having too much fun." Neither one of us had any type of tennis skills. We only took the class for fun and exercise. Consequently, we had a blast together. Trellis is a beautiful woman. She is fair skinned with light brown hair with a golden tint in it. She has a bright personality and dresses in fun unique styles that matches her personality in a noticeable way. She laughs with a cadence that makes you want to join in on whatever she finds humorous. Trellis has a warm demeanor but at times can go into her shell of protection. She loves hard and has a kind heart. Trellis and I met on the tennis courts in college. Our laughter connected our passion for life. Our friendship was solidified over a pan of flaky biscuits and sausage when she invited me to her apartment for lunch. I was in awe with the fact that she lived by herself, went to college and had a job working as a cashier at a local grocery store. All she didn't have at the time was a car; all I didn't have at the time was an apartment. She loved Mickey Mouse and I loved Kermit and Miss Piggy. Together, we loved food, a lot! She dreamed of being a mom. I wanted to create human change in our society. We both wanted to be wealthy enough to shop for whatever fashions we desired. We began to discuss the possibility of becoming roommates. I continued to save my money and shop for things I wanted for my new place.

My Independent Journey

Interesting

Trellis and I looked around until we found an apartment that sat on a hillside overlooking a view of the freeway. The opposite of the freeway was filled with homes and upscale apartments. We thought we were the stuff! Trellis gave one month's notice in her apartment. By this time my closet was completely filled with everything I needed to move out. I had saved up enough money for at least two months' rent.

After a few months, I had the talk with dad and told him I was moving out soon. During our talk, dad asked me why I thought it was a good idea to move out. I told him I wanted my independence, my own space, and to be free to set my own educational goals without worrying about meeting his expectations. Then he told me if I leave, I cannot come back home. I would have to figure out how to manage my life without the financial support toward my education. He told me it would be expensive to live on my own without a higher paying job. I understood everything he said and thanked him for the talk. When the conversation replayed in my mind, I worried about him saying I could never come back home. What if I can't make it? What if my new roommate doesn't work out? What if I get homesick? However, I was determined to make it work and prove a point to my dad. The time had come for me to start my own journey. I was venturing off from the only pathway of the journey I knew and loved. I was taking with me every lesson I learned, and every moment I treasured, good or bad.

As I packed my bags in preparation to execute my plan, I made space for my life essentials. I knew I was as prepared as I could be at that time. I was most excited about how my mom would feel about my decision. I wanted her to know I heard her voice of wisdom. While I knew how much she loved my dad, I also knew how much she depended on him in ways she didn't want me to ever depend on a man. Mom once shared with me that she felt she owed my dad a lifetime commitment of appreciation because he literally helped save her life. She knew if she had not met and married him, she might have died a long time ago. Her medical condition was so dire until the doctors told her that without getting a stoma, she had no chance of living. Dad's influence on saving her life came at a time when she was too sick to make the decision on her own will. However, she told me all she prayed for every day after that was for God to let her live long enough to see all her children's children. She lived every day of her life for her family. She wasn't living life to the fullest for herself. I continued to prepare to move out. Trellis had become a part of our family by now. I changed my degree course to human behavior and continued to work with Mary Ellen until I graduated and got a new job in the field of my degree.

A lot was happening in the McGee household. My brother went on to play professional football with the Buffalo Bills. He was on the pathway to fulfill his dream and keep the promise to buy mom a red corvette and a new house.

A year passed. One day, out of the blue my brother called me from Buffalo to ask me to pick up his girlfriend, Sherri, from the airport. He had met her while in college at Michigan State. Leroy went on to describe what she looked like starting with her 20" waist, and hourglass figure. I asked him again, "What does she look like?" He said, "Pretty." He gave me the flight information and told me he was flying in from Buffalo the next day and would pick her up at my apartment. I was in a panic because I was pushing almost 200 lbs. I didn't want to meet my brother's girlfriend looking like a stuffed pig. I tried on different outfits trying to shave away at least ten pounds. Nothing was working. Finally, I gave up and accepted the fact that she was going to make her own judgment about me no matter what weight I was. Trellis and I picked Sherri up and we immediately made a connection. The way my brother described her was spot on, except, she wasn't just pretty. She was a beautiful lady with a captivating smile of pearly white, straight teeth. She was near perfect looking to a sister who was carrying a ridiculous amount of weight around my thighs and waistline from a diet of cheese Doritos and tuna fish, biscuits and sausage.

Dream Deferred

My brother and Sherri continued their long-distance relationship after she went back to Michigan for over a year. Then, Leroy suffered a terrible knee injury and was put on injured reserves. Then one day, I heard someone yelling my name from the parking lot of our apartment complex. I ran out to the balcony and there stood Leroy. He was standing right outside of his black RX7 sports car, wearing black leather pants and a jacket. For a moment I thought he might have been Eddie Murphy stopping by to invite me to his stand-up comedy show. Leroy waved for me to come down. I ran down as fast as I could. As I got closer, I noticed the expression on his face didn't match the excitement I thought he would have seeing me. I asked what's wrong? He told me he had been released from the Buffalo Bills because his rehab doctor told him he might not be able to play again. His dreams were shattered but the thing that bothered him the most was that he wouldn't be able to get mom that red corvette and a big house. I was speechless. Leroy had come to me for support. Then I remembered one of my life's essential lessons. When something is unexpectedly taken from you that you worked hard for, don't give up looking for something better in return. I told him, "Mom will be ok as long as she knows you are ok. A car and a house are material things, they can be replaced. You are her only son you can't." We both stood in silence for an emotional moment before he sped off burning rubber. I stood frozen in time until he disappeared from my sight. I cried hard for him but prayed harder for God to restore his spirit. This was the beginning of my independent life journey and it was hard for me to see my brother hurting like that.

I moved out at age 18. Fast forward to my life at age 28. I lived in LA for almost two years. I would come back and forth from LA to visit with my family. My brother and his wife Sherri would let my niece Natasha go back with me to spend some weekends. I thought she was my daughter. Everyone said she looked like me. That was all I needed to take over being front and center in her young life. It had to have bothered Sherri, but she never let me know it. She pacified my co-parenting invasion with grace.

I moved back to San Diego after dissolving a bad relationship. I was broken and mad at the world. So, I went back to school to fulfill my educational goal of becoming a therapist for the deaf and hard of hearing. Or to become a psychologist to write children's books to help them heal from racial issues as I had growing up. I moved in with my brother and his wife until I saved up enough money to get my own place. A coworker named Julie told me that her brother had invested in an apartment complex in San Diego, so I moved in there. It wasn't a good neighborhood, but I needed to be on my own.

Future Husband

I moved into a roach-infested, one-bedroom apartment downstairs. I had never seen roaches that big in my life! UGH! I learned how to deal with them, all while hoping to get a better paying job and be able to move out sooner than later. I was there for about a month, when I saw two Black men moving in upstairs. One was friendly and quite personable. He was small in stature with a charming smile and enormous brown eyes. I often heard the other man call him "Bugs", which made me chuckle inside. Bugs always spoke when both of them passed by my living room window on their way to their apartment. The other man was tall and had an incredible muscular build. He had a large red afro and wore blue jean overalls with a skintight, long sleeved shirt under them. He was very light skinned with the fullest lips I had ever seen on a Black man. He never spoke. I deemed him extremely overconfident.

I finally asked Bugs, "Does your friend talk?" He laughed.

"Ohhh yes, that's my cousin and he talked my ear off all the way from Illinois to San Diego! He said his name is CB."

"Is that his real name?" I asked.

"No, it's Charles. But everyone calls him CB," Bugs said.

One day, CB decided to speak when I was on my way to my daily jog. He asked me what I was going to do when I got back. I thought it really wasn't none of his business. However, I answered, "Cook me some fried chicken for dinner." He asked if I would fry some for him too. I gasped and told him if he wanted some fried chicken, he had to buy his own because I wasn't sharing my chicken with him! He said "OK" and took off in his car. By the time I returned from my jog he was waiting at my front door with two plump chicken breasts. Dinner was great, so he said.

A few days later we were talking outside my front door. He asked why I wasn't in a relationship. I explained to him that I was done with men for a while and that all I wanted to do was be the baddest bachelorette in San Diego. For now, I was concentrating on getting through school. Being in a relationship or even marriage was not an option for me for a long time.

"How do you know your future husband isn't standing in front of you right now?" He replied.

"HA, HA! No way," I said. Two years later we were married and welcomed my only birth son to our marriage, Chasman. Six months later, my son, Charles Jr. and my son Kenneth seven years later. I'll share the details of this amazing family journey in my next book, *Destiny Awaits*.

Moving on Up to The Hillside

Dad was a ham operator and wanted to move to a larger home to set up a ham radio room. He also wanted to buy a larger home for his growing family. He looked for a home outside of town so he could have open air space to set up a mega sized antenna on top of his home. When he found the one that he wanted, the homeowner's association told him he couldn't put up his antenna, so he retracted his offer. Nothing was going to stop him from finding the home of his dreams with enough property and open air space for his antenna. When he finally found the perfect home, it was beautiful! It overlooked all of the East County and was big enough for our whole growing family to spend our Thanksgiving, Christmas, and every holiday we wanted to with our parents. When he bought his home Leroy, Esther and I had all moved out leaving my Baby Sister at home with our parents. Mom was fine with having my Baby Sister there for as long as she wanted. She didn't encourage her to go off to college. Mom didn't want to lose her baby daughter. Dad was immersed in his new job at Miramar and working on attaining his master's degree in business administration. It took effortless coordination for all of us to come together to spend quality time with each other. We'd pack our weekend travel bags and each take a 20-minute or less drive to pile into my parent's home to spend fun loving time together. We enjoyed every minute, all the while, regretting the moment when we had to go back to our separate lives away from each other. We had grown to love and respect the synergy of the McGee Family. I never wanted to let it go.

Live and Learn

I made mistakes and certainly disappointed my parents in ways that they must have never imagined. They always let me know that no matter what they would always love me. The expectation was for me to grow and learn from every mistake and bad decision I made, even if it smashed my pride to pieces to admit it.

I never thought that I would be able to capture the essence of how I feel about my parents. The truth of the matter is that I could continue to share with you who they were to me for the rest of my life. However, it is time for me to share with you how I chose to live my life out with every intentional effort to become the woman they would be Godly proud of.

I often thought I might have blown it at times, but my shortcomings were always supported by the grace of God, the unconditional love from mom and the voice of wisdom from dad. Again, my parents weren't perfect, but they were amazing to me. For sure I disagreed with them and became mad at them for reasons that I felt were unjust. However, I had to depend on God and reason with myself to make things right within my own heart. Sometimes the disappointment with my parents lasted longer than it should have. But in the end, I always took note of how they continued to give me guidance and nurture me. No one has to share my perspective to who my parents were to me but me. I just pray that you can appreciate how I chose to express it to you. I had to find a way to hold them in everlasting memory and a way for me to move beyond the hurt and pain of them not being physically here with me anymore. I know there are millions of children who feel similar to the way I do about my parents. I also know there are others who can't even mention their parents name without a repulsive feeling. I hope one day they find a way to forgive their parents and see something good at the core of who they are that allows them to freely acknowledge some love for their parents and be blessed in return by doing so.

I Grew A Field of Love for My Parents

Flowers are beautiful. They create a colorful picture against natures' earthly backdrop of green grass, tall trees and mountains that canvas the blue skyline. When flowers grow, they bloom only during their season of life. Even flowers that grow annually still go dormant for a time before they continue their life cycle. When I behold the breathtaking beauty of a flower, I think about God's purpose for even creating them. Every flower has a purpose and a life cycle that offers something significant to the ecology of the earth right down to the tiniest insect. Picking a flower cuts off its lifeline and even putting it in a vase of water doesn't allow it to live out its intended life cycle. Soon it will begin to droop over and wither into a less attractive sight and will lose its fragrant smell. So, instead of growing flowers to give to my parents, throughout my life I grew a field of love, honor and respect. It lives in and out of season and never dies. It's rooted in the nurtured soil of God's commandment to honor thy parents. Every day I walk through the field and pick a basket full of love, honor or respect and I proudly handed it to them with heartfelt appreciation. The field grew more and more until it consumed my being. So much that I ended up simply presenting myself to them throughout their lifetime. Now that both of my parents are with each other in heaven, I still find myself walking through the field, picking out a bouquet. I wanted to share a symbol of my appreciation for the journey I have been on and I found a way to do so through this book. Please find someone you feel deserves to be loved, honored and respected and share this book from my heart to theirs. Life is too short not to.

THE END...for now.

IN LOVING MEMORY OF
EDDIE MAE MCGEE (1937-2000)
AND
WILLIE JAMES MCGEE (1935-2020)

ACKNOWLEDGEMENTS

Width deep love and appreciation in my heart, I give all honor to my Lord and Savior Jesus Christ for blessing me with the vision and the strength to make this book a reality. First, I want to acknowledge my family and say thank you:

To my husband Charles Burton, Sr. ("CB"), whose daily patience and support were incredible during the process of writing this book.

To my sons, Charles Jr., Kenneth, and Chasman, and my Goddaughter Everlena, for giving me the love and support I needed from you to complete my dream. Chasman, your excitement for this book pushed me on a daily to the finish line!

To all my grandchildren, this book was written for you to share with your children's children and beyond!

To my brother, Leroy, you encouraged me to share my story on behalf of our parent's incredible legacy and the loving respect you have for them.

To my sisters Esther and Baby Sister, because of the love you have for our parents, you gave me the unspoken needed support at a critical time during this process.

To my sister-in-law Sherri, you gave your heart to my parents by affectionately calling them mom and dad and treating them as such.

To my nieces, Natasha and Ashley, and my Nephew Roy, your presence always gives me loving support.

To all my sisters' children, thank you for sharing a part of your journey with me.

To my Aunt Marie, you kept me intrigued with details from my mom's side of the family.

To my Aunt Mary Frances, you gave me thoughtful insight into my dad's childhood years.

To my cousin Frank and his daughter Lisa, all I can say is thank you for always being you!

I also want to thank the following people:

My spiritual mentor, Mother Hooks ("Lady Jo"). You have always believed in me and supported me publicly with this book on your talk show.

My three undeniable friends for life--Meredith, my prayer and shopping partner. Trellis, my 1st roommate, and my children's Godmother. Sister Criss, who called me almost every day in anticipation of the completion of this book, always sharing heartfelt laughter and support.

Verena, you always check in with me just because that's what you do!

Alberto, Daniel, and their families, thank you for always being there to offer your support and adoration.

Jimmy, my friend who always shares reflective conversations of us growing up together.

Saul, my graphic artist, you simply rock! Working with you and my husband to capture my complicated vision for my book cover was intense, but the outcome is amazing. You are the best at what you do.

Finally, thank you to my incredible editor KishaLynn Elliott. You completely blew me away with your "grit and grind it out" support. It brought me to this point of telling everyone who picks this book up, "if you desire to become an author, do it with KishaLynn! You will be amazed at her skillful professionalism."

To all the rest of you, whatever journey you are on, I thank God we have crossed paths along the way.

Be Blessed Always,

Cynthia McGee Burton

‍‍

ABOUT THE AUTHOR

C ynthia McGee Burton, M.A., was born in Honolulu, Hawaii. She is the proud sister of her beloved older brother and two younger sisters. She has been a national trainer, motivational speaker, and facilitator for 38 years. She has been married to her devoted husband Charles "CB" Burton for 35 years and counting. They live in San Diego, California, and share three incredible sons and seven beautiful grandchildren. In 2018, Cynthia retired from working in the educational field for over 43 years. She is the author of two Mayor's Award youth development programs—*Academic Success Apprenticeship Program* and *Community Youth Leadership Alliance. A Phenomenal Journey* is the first book of stories from her personal life. She is currently working on the sequel, *Destiny Awaits*, which continues the journey.

Cynthia has worked locally and nationally in the urban faith community as a ministry youth leader and family life coach for almost four decades. Cynthia co-founded Centered Life Ministries Inc. in 2015. She is an ordained Missionary, the owner of The Royaltea Garden and The Restoration Tea Room for urban families. She currently co-hosts the podcast "Cross-Generational Voices" with JoAnne "Lady Jo" Smith Hooks on KEPX Radio and works as a Restorative Consciousness independent consultant. She is a former recipient of the Channel 10 Leadership Award for being the founder of the first Gospel Signing Choir of San Diego.

Made in the USA
Las Vegas, NV
28 April 2021

22150142R00102